Follyfoot Remembered

The Follyfoot cast – left to right – Slugger (Arthur English) – Steve (Steve Hodson) – Ron (Christian Rodska) – The Colonel (Desmond Llewelyn) – Dora (Gillian Blake)

Follyfoot Remembered

Jane Royston
Horse Manager

DERWEN PUBLISHING
Pembroke · Dyfed

ACKNOWLEDGEMENTS

Thank you to everyone who encouraged me to tell my story.

Ray: for your support, advice and friendship, in the producing of this book.

Christine: for allowing access to your photographs and your scrap book.

Steve: for providing some personal photographs.

Ray and Lucille: for your support.

Michael and John: for all your time helping with the computer and organising the specimen copy for the publishers.

James: for your help with the YTV photo archive.

Peter Grant: for making Ray and I so welcome at Stockeld Park during our research.

Special thanks to **Gillian, Steve, Paul**, **Christian** and **Gillian Bush-Bailey** who agreed to be interviewed by Ray.

Thank you to the artistes and crew, too numerous to name who also contributed to the book.

Copyright © 2011 Jane Royston and Ray Knight

The rights of Jane Royston and Ray Knight to be identified as authors of this work have been asserted in accordance with the Copyright, Designs and Patents Act 1988.

First published in Great Britain by Derwen Publishing 2011.

This book is copyright under the Berne Convention.
Apart from fair dealing for the purposes of research or private study, or criticism or review, as permitted under the Copyright, Designs and Patents Act 1988, no part of this publication may be reproduced, stored or transmitted in any form or by any means without prior written permission from the publishers, or in the case of reprographic reproduction in accordance with the terms of licences issued by the Copyright Licensing Agency. Enquiries concerning reproduction outside these terms should be sent to the publishers at the following address.

Derwen Publishing,
3 Bengal Villas,
Pembroke, Dyfed,
Wales, SA71 4BH

A CIP catalogue for this book is available from the British Library.

ISBN 978-1-907084-05-8

The authors have used their best efforts in preparing this book, and the information included herein. Where practical they have made contact with known surviving members of the cast and production team. The authors apologise if in their research efforts they have omitted or been unable to contact some people mentioned in the book. They make no representation or warranties with respect to the accuracy or completeness of the contents of this book.

Design and production by David Porteous Editions.
www.davidporteous.com

Printed in Hong Kong by Great Wall Press.

Dedication

This book is dedicated to the late **Tony Essex**, Executive Producer, my 'boss' and good friend who gave me the opportunity to live a dream. I would also like to remember all the Follyfoot cast and crew, including those who sadly are no longer with us.

Contents

The Very Beginning	8
Follyfoot Remembered James Bolam	9
My Follyfoot Journey Begins	10
My Journey with Hollin Hall	12
The Settlers	14
My Dream Becomes a Reality	16

SERIES ONE

Episode 1: Dora	18
Episode 2: Steve	21
In Conversation with Paul Guess	23
Episode 3: Gypsy	25
Episode 4: Shadow	27
Episode 5: One White-Foot Charley	29
Episode 6: The Charity Horse	30
Episode 7: Know-All's-Nag	31
Episode 8: Moonstone	32
In Conversation with Gillian Bush-Bailey	34
Episode 9: Stryker's Good Deed	36
Episode 10: Mr. She-Knows	37
Follyfoot Remembered: Hazel Cleasson	39
Episode 11: The Standstill Horse	41
Episode 12: Birthday at Follyfoot	42
Follyfoot Remembered: Allan Pyrah	44
Episode 13: A Day in the Sun	45
Moving to Winter Quarters	46
In Conversation with Christian Rodska	47

SERIES TWO

Episode 1: Someone, Somewhere	52
Episode 2: The Debt	54
Episode 3: Family of Strangers	56
Episode 4: Present for Sandy	57
Episode 5: The Innocents	59

Episode 6: The Hundred Pound Horse	62
Episode 7: Poor Bald Head	64
Episode 8: The Prize	66
Episode 9: Treasure Hunt	68
Episode 10: Debt of Honour	70
Episode 11: Out-of-the-Blue Horse	72
Episode 12: The Awakening	74
Follyfoot Remembered: Anthony Andrews	76
Episode 13: Fly Away Home	77
In Conversation with Steve Hodson	80

SERIES THREE

Episode 1: The Distant Voice	86
Episode 2: The Four-Legged Hat	88
Follyfoot Remembered: John Cater	90
Episode 3: Barney	92
Episode 4: Miss Him When He's Gone	94
Follyfoot Remembered: Richard Beaumont	96
Episode 5: The Dream	97
Episode 6: The Challenge	99
Episode 7: The Letter	101
Follyfoot Remembered: Tracy Eddon	103
Episode 8: The Bridge Builder	104
Follyfoot Remembered: Mervyn Cumming	107
Episode 9: Uncle Joe	109
Episode 10: The Helping Hand	111
Episode 11: Rain on Friday	113
Episode 12: Hazel	114
Episode 13: Walk in the Wood	116
In Conversation with Gillian Blake	119
37 Years Later	123
Radio Leeds	125
Arthur English Remembered	126
Desmond Llewelyn Remembered	127
Photograph Credits	128
Afterword	128

The Very Beginning

LET me introduce myself to you, I am Jane Royston, the lucky person who was horse manager on the award-winning Yorkshire Television (YTV) series Follyfoot. My early life was one of a great love of horses. I played truant from school in order to compete in horse trials, hunt, and spend all my time with these beautiful animals.

I left school, after not having attended very much as I regularly played truant and went up to the local stables where my horse Lita Rosa was kept. When my school report came one term my mother noticed the entry, 'Jane would do better if she was at school more often'. She 'blew a fuse!' and deciding that there was no money to be made from working with horses I was packed off to secretarial college. But after only two terms there I was brought into the family business, the West Riding Hotel in Leeds. I did not work very hard there. My dad was either very understanding or had completely given up on me. At lunch times I frequently went to the Mansion (a famous restaurant in Roundhay Park, Leeds) to meet my grandma. I also happened to meet several businessmen of Leeds, one of whom had a friend who had started to work at Yorkshire Television as a press officer.

Jane with Sky

One day, the press officer told me about a producer from Yorkshire Television, who was filming a children's television series called *Tom Grattan's War* and who needed someone to help the leading actress with her horse riding – was I interested? Of course I was!

I was given three different appointments to meet the producer, Tony Essex at Yorkshire Television's temporary headquarters next door to the new studio complex which was still being completed, but each time he cancelled. He then suggested I should go to his house. I remember the occasion well. I had been to the stables that morning and ridden my horse Sky and, therefore, I probably smelt of horses. I thought; 'never mind, he will have to accept me just as I am', which he did; he was very nice, especially as he offered me the job. He asked me how much I earned at my present job, I told him and he said no, he could not possibly pay me that amount. Help, what was I to do now? I could not possibly work for less. He then told me his suggested amount: to which I replied: "that's too much". He just laughed and told me he would have the contract drawn up.

So, at the age of 23 this was the beginning of my journey with Yorkshire Television and Tony Essex.

YTV Studios

Tony Essex and Monica Dickens

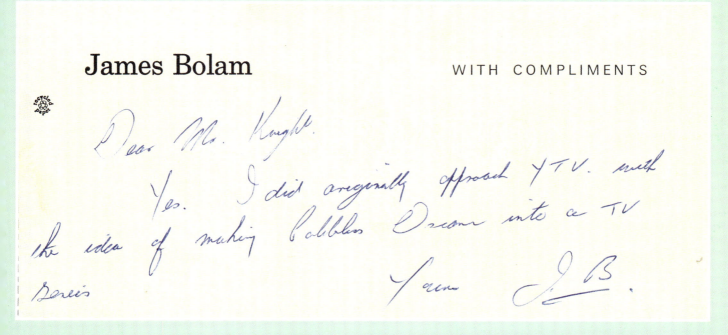

James Bolam, MBE is a well-respected English actor and singer, who originally suggested to Yorkshire Television the idea of making Cobbler's Dream *into a TV series.*

My Follyfoot Journey Begins

Time had passed since *Tom Grattan's War* had been televised. My father had retired and sold the family business, and now I had to go into the big wide world and earn my own living in order to afford to keep my new horse – Austrian Sky.

I joined the E. J. Arnold printing company in Leeds, where I became a VDU operator. One day my boss said I had received a phone call. This was not allowed, and I thought I would be in big trouble, but for some reason my boss was quite amicable about it. He said it was from Tony Essex of Yorkshire Television. When I spoke to Tony he mentioned a book called *Cobbler's Dream*, which he would like me to read as soon as possible. I went to the studios and met Tony, who gave me the book, and he told me he wanted to make it into a children's television series. Despite my lifelong love of horses I had never read the book, which was by the famous author Monica Dickens, the great-granddaughter of Victorian novelist Charles Dickens. I rather cheekily told Tony I thought the book had possibilities as a children's TV series!

Tony Essex had many meetings with Donald Baverstock, who was the then Director of Programmes, and other members of the YTV management team about the series, as this was going to cost them and the associated German television company, Tele-Munich, a great deal of money.

It was only a few days before I got another call from Tony, asking me to meet him at the studios that evening; he said he had something important to tell me. When I arrived Tony said, 'Let's go to the bar, we have something to celebrate'. He had received the go-ahead to make the series. The studio bar was to become an important part of my life and over the next few years I would meet many famous celebrities and stars there.

The budget had been calculated and now the real work had to begin. I asked Tony who was going to be in charge of the horses. He replied, 'Who do you think – YOU!' I truly could not believe it.

I worked my notice at E. J. Arnold and with great excitement, and a feeling of apprehension, started work at Yorkshire Television.

Tony told me he did not know what name to give the series – he had decided he would not call it *Cobbler's Dream*. Then he had a brainwave. He gave his daughter Tamara a map of Yorkshire and asked her to select a name at random from the map. She pointed her finger at a village called Follifoot, near Harrogate. Tony then changed the middle letter *i* to *y* and Follyfoot was born.

I was working at Yorkshire Television in Alan Whicker's office, which was next door to Tony's. Tony called me into his office and told me how worried he was because the Location Manager could not find a suitable location. Could I help?

Oh dear! I was going to have to tell Tony about my secret hideaway,

The bulldozers move in at Hollin Hall

Work in progress at Hollin Hall

Hollin Hall, which I always imagined I was going to run away to whenever my parents threatened to sell my horse, Austrian Sky. I told Tony the whole story and he promised that I would not lose Sky even if he had to buy her for me. Tony took his daughter to see the farm, which was to become the home of Follyfoot. He saw the potential and fell in love with it straightaway. He felt it was the ideal location.

Yorkshire Television, and the agent for the Harewood Estate, drew up a detailed contract that specified where we could film and what we could do to the farm and its buildings. It ensured that we did not damage any trees or interfere with any birds or their nests, nor must we prevent public access over the footpaths and bridleways. This was not very convenient as they crossed between the farmhouse and the stables. On a few occasions we had to persuade riders and walkers to take an alternative route. The contract also ruled out any fishing in the estate lake, though I'm not sure that was always observed!

Permission was given by the Earl of Harewood, who owned the property and within days the bulldozers had moved in. Stables were built, sets and living quarters were made in the house for the 'Horse Girls' as we became known; and the barn became the home of wardrobe, canteen and make-up. It is amazing, all these years later, to recall that the entire construction costs were so little, apparently well under £10,000! Similar to the cost of making each episode which usually took 7-10 days

The Lightning tree lands

to rehearse and film and only 3-4 minutes per day of film were used.

The Lightning Tree was the idea of Tony Essex. It would fill a space which, from the cameraman's point of view, was featureless. The tree, which had really been struck by lightning, was found about half-a-mile away and was moved by a 20-ton crane and put into position in seven tons of concrete. The tree became a focal point for the series; the signature tune was named after it, and Dora treated it as if it had magical powers.

Before we started filming the *News of the World* newspaper came up with an exclusive scoop from somewhere, and reported that three young girls were living alone on a remote film set in Yorkshire, and 'was this proper?' Tony had to advertise for a live-in male caretaker to oversee site security. As it turned out he was not live-in and we hardly ever saw him!

Hollin Hall had become Follyfoot Farm, and was now ready to become a filming and living set.

Horse girls can turn their hand to anything. Janet, Karen and Gillian.

My Journey with Hollin Hall

I really feel that Hollin Hall, which is situated on the Harewood Estate, and the future home of *Follyfoot*, deserves a mention as it has a very special meaning in my life. It all began in the winter of 1964 on a very cold but bright day. I was out hunting on my first horse, Lita Rosa, when we came upon a deserted farmhouse and barns in a beautiful setting, situated by a lake and surrounded by woods. The house was falling down and in need of much love and attention, the barns were also in need of repair and the yard was very overgrown. Only the barn at the top of the yard, which had straw down on the floor, seemed to be in use for the farm animals to take shelter.

After seeing Hollin Hall for the first time I felt drawn to the place, and would often hack over there and just halt my horse by the lake and go into a dream world of my own; wondering what it used to be like and also who had lived there. I used to imagine myself living there with my horses, never dreaming that one day I would – and also work for Yorkshire Television. How lucky can one get?

I hope when you read the rest of the book you will grow to love Hollin Hall, now renamed Follyfoot Farm, as much as I did, because to me it will always be a very magical place.

Hollin Hall before renovation

Hollin Hall as Follyfoot Farm

The Stables at Follyfoot Farm

The Settlers

The Settlers – from left to right – Mike Jones, Geoffrey Srodzinski, John Fyffe and Cindy Kent

The Settlers were a folk pop group who recorded the theme tune to Follyfoot, which you can hear at the beginning and end of each episode.

The Lightning Tree, was written by Francis Essex, brother of executive producer Tony, under the pen name of Stephen Francis, and was released as a single in 1971, reaching number 36 in the UK singles chart.

The Follyfoot cast with The Settlers

My Dream Becomes a Reality

Before any of the filming started my first job was to organise horses for the publicity photo shoots, which were taken at Mount Pleasant Stud, Scarcroft, not far from the *Follyfoot* location. I had kept my horses there for many years. We used a mare and foal and also my horse, Sky. She eventually became the horse on the cover of the television tie-in reprint of *Cobbler's Dream*. Gillian Blake, who had been cast as the heroine Dora, had a ride on Sky, which really was a little unfair on her, as Sky very often had a mind of her own, but Gillian coped really well.

I now had to find the horses that would live at Follyfoot, and a suitable one for Gillian to ride. On one of Monica Dickens' early visits to the *Follyfoot* location she mentioned that her sister-in-law Jeanne-Marie Dickens, Countess Wenckheim, had a mare called Flash which she thought we could only use for the initial filming as the Countess wanted to put the mare in foal later in the year. The only problem was Flash was somewhere in acres of fields on a farm near Castle Howard. Mel, one of the Grips on the film crew, drove the *Follyfoot* horsebox and said he would take me to pick up Flash. This was easier said than done. Flash did not want to be caught; the chance of being a film star did not seem to interest her. It took three of us two hours to catch her and load her into the horsebox. As we were on our way back to Follyfoot, crossing Lendal bridge in York, the horsebox engine decided it was not going any further. Luckily Mel soon got the problem sorted out and we eventually got back home to Follyfoot. What a day!

While I was on the hunt for horses I met the Edwards sisters (Ann and Vicky), who had a trekking centre in Pateley Bridge (Eagle Hall). They were willing to come and work at Follyfoot and provide us with horses. This was really good news, and a relief as I knew their horses would be well behaved because they had been used in the trekking centre.

In the middle of hiring all the horses I got an urgent phone call from Tony Essex; would I go and see him straight away, it was very important. When I got there, he told me I had nearly brought the programme to a standstill by finding the horses for the series on my own. The unions said that a horse was a prop and therefore it was the job of the props buyer. As a newcomer to the world of television I felt this was ridiculous and told Tony so in no uncertain terms. To solve the problem he asked if I would compromise and take the props buyer with me. I had no choice but to agree. The props buyer was a great guy, Rod Saul, who was actually very understanding and helpful and we became good friends. In fact his daughter, Christine, eventually came to work with the horses.

I now had the horse for Gillian to ride, and also the horses for the yard shots and some of the riding scenes. The Edwards sisters and I were now living full time at Follyfoot and getting ready to shoot the first episode.

Me moving in

Flash with our friend Susan

Christine on dart removal duty

Series 1

Episode 1   Dora
Episode 2   Steve
Episode 3   Gypsy
Episode 4   Shadow
Episode 5   One White-Foot Charley
Episode 6   The Charity Horse
Episode 7   Know All's Nag
Episode 8   Moonstone
Episode 9   Stryker's Good Deed
Episode 10   Mr She-Knows
Episode 11   The Standstill Horse
Episode 12   Birthday at Follyfoot
Episode 13   A Day in the Sun

Episode 1: Dora

Directed by Stephen Frears

The Story

Dora (Gillian Blake) is a lonely rich girl whose parents do not try to understand her and leave her behind with her uncle, the Colonel (Desmond Llewelyn), for a year. Dora loves horses and goes out for a ride and meets the Night Riders, which leads to a terrifying experience and her first meeting with Steve (Steve Hodson). The Colonel tells Dora about Follyfoot Farm and suggests she rides over there where she meets Slugger (Arthur English), Ron Stryker (Christian Rodska) and the horses which have been taken in because of bad treatment or old age.

This is the beginning of a whole new life for Dora.

My Story

It was 6am. I had woken up first and shouted out to the girls to rise and shine; it was a lovely day and time to get up. I stayed in bed until the girls were dressed and on their way out to feed, water and muck out the horses. I then got up and exercised the horses required for filming, groomed or sometimes bathed them.

In this episode we also needed horses for the Night Riders, which would have to be trained to lie down as if dead. I remember when I read the script I panicked, thinking how on earth am I going to achieve this and thought maybe I should not be doing this job. Tony had luckily arranged for a well-known stunt coordinator, Peter Diamond, to direct these scenes. Peter also organised the stunt guys and the horses. I felt very privileged to work with him and tried to learn as much as I could from Peter.

The opening scene of *Follyfoot* was at a location called Stockeld Park near Spofforth.

I knew the location because it was where I stayed and trained with the Bramham Moor Pony Club Event Team. The opening shot was of the Colonel riding through the gateway over a cattle grid – phew! It could have been nasty but that was the only way we could get the shot the Director, Stephen Frears, wanted;

Stockeld Park

and what the director wanted, within reason, we had to achieve. We had to lay boards down over the grid and the Colonel's horse managed to get across safely.

The next shot of the horses was taken from inside the house up the wonderful main staircase, which Tony Essex had fallen in love with. He insisted it was used for filming Dora looking out of the window at the horses grazing in the field. To get the shot the horses were led to the field and placed in position. As soon as 'action' was called, food was put on the ground, head collars were taken off, and the Horse Girls ran out of shot. Usually this little trick worked with the horses. If it had not we would have been in trouble, as the field was very large and had lots of lovely grass in it.

The stable scenes where Dora is introduced to Dragon (Flash) were very easy and Dragon took to the cameras, lights and crew as if she had done it all her life.

The next day we were filming in a field near the river at East Keswick. Peter Diamond, now with the help of the stunt guys, took over. When the Night Riders first caught the horses there was a white one that bucked and really tried to get his rider off. This had the Horse Girls killing themselves with laughter. Peter Jackson (Lighting Cameraman) took some lovely shots of Dora riding through the river and in the woods, making it look quite romantic.

One of the required shots was of Dora being chased into the river and up the bank by the Night Riders. The Director decided he wanted the shot taken from Dora's angle. The Cameraman, Graham Barker, said he would do it and for this he had to get in front of the stuntman on the horse, carry a camera and film while the

Dora riding Dragon (Flash)

Graham Barker's first horse ride!

stuntman steered the cantering horse. A Cameraman will really do anything to get a good shot. Graham had never been on a horse before.

We hired specially-trained stunt horses for the Night Riders as they were required in the storyline to lie down as if wounded.

The ground was raked free of stones and long, green grass laid down to make it softer for when they went down; this was done because if the horse had hurt itself it would be very reluctant to do it again. The stunt horse trainer was always close by while the actors did their scenes. Sometimes the horses did try to get up and the shot had to be re-taken. At no time were the horses panicked.

On a lot of the horse chase scenes more than one camera would be used, and they were placed at different angles because some of the shots could only be done in one take. This was due to the time factor and the complexity of the shots – especially the Night Rider scenes.

Dora, riding Dragon, sees Follyfoot Farm for the first time and meets Ron and Slugger and, of course, the horse residents. I know how she must have felt. The first time I saw Hollin Hall as Follyfoot Farm, after the restoration work and the horses moved in, was a dream come true for me. When Dora met the horses in the stables we had a horse girl behind each one to push them to the front of the stable and we also made sure the actors always had a pocket full of pony nuts.

Night Riders

Preparing the ground

Dora's first view of Follyfoot Farm

Episode 2: Steve

Directed by Frederic Goode

The Story

Steve, after being sacked by the Squire (William Mervyn) for supposedly being one of the Night Riders, goes to Follyfoot Farm to see the Colonel about a horse that was injured during the chase. Dora finds Steve in the barn and says she will help him get the lame horse back to Follyfoot Farm. Dora and Steve have to cross a river to get away from the Squire's men, who will probably put the horse down because he is lame. The Night Riders come to Follyfoot Farm and let the horses out including Folly the foal. In the end the horse is saved and Folly is found and, best of all, the Colonel takes Steve on to work with Dora at Follyfoot, to help look after Dora's Collection.

Steve is caught with the pony

My Story

The star of this episode was a horse called Kip, which belonged to Janet Harrison, one of the Horse Girls. Janet just rode up to the farm and asked if we needed any more horse staff. She said she could get hold of horses for filming as her parents had a livery yard just down the Harrogate Road. I asked her if she had a horse that did not mind water and could swim. She said yes the one she was riding – Kip. I immediately said I would ring Tony Essex and see if we could give her a job looking after the horses. Janet joined us and Kip became the star of this episode, the horse Steve was trying to save.

Kip was actually lame in both front feet as he had navicular, a painful condition of the foot, but he was specially shod and the vet said he could be used for light riding. It was a bitterly cold and wet day for Kip's starring role; the swim across the river that was shot at Bolton Abbey. Janet was asked to try the pony in the water first before Gillian and Steve did the actual shot. They, unlike Janet, were wearing wetsuits to protect them from the cold. All went well until Kip decided he would not go any further and turned back to the bank. It was decided to go for a take with Steve and Gillian but again Kip turned round, so the shot was cut. Everybody went to the other side of the river and were just filmed walking out.

I have to admit you would not have got me going into the river like Gillian and Steve did. Gillian was actually kicked by accident while swimming, but still carried on even though she was in pain. The reason Kip kept turning round, we found out afterwards, was because of undercurrents, which we did not realise were there. Kip may have stopped a serious accident from happening.

When I was recently talking to Steve Hodson about this episode he told me how two members of the crew, Mel and John, came to his rescue when he was caught in the undercurrent and he felt that if they had not, he might not now be around to tell the story.

Folly the foal came from a very good Welsh pony stud at Beckwithshaw and was bred from show stock. I think the owner, Mrs Towers, was a little afraid that something might happen to the foal, which was worth a lot of money. So after the shot of the foal being found loose in the woods she would not let us use her again; even though we really did take good care of her. A new Folly had to be found and bought. Sadly she was a darker grey and not as good looking, but never mind – it sort of worked.

Steve and Kip in the river

In Conversation with Paul Guess (Lewis Hammond)

PAUL APPEARED IN THE FOLLOWING EPISODES – ALL FROM FIRST SERIES:

DORA
Directed by Stephen Frears

STEVE
Directed by Frederick Goode

SHADOW
Directed by Frederick Goode

ONE WHITE FOOT CHARLEY
Directed by Ian McFarlane

THE STANDSTILL HORSE
Directed by Ian McFarlane

How did you get the part of Lewis, and where did you audition?
I auditioned in London for Stephen Frears as I recall events - I had worked for him previously so he knew of my abilities and I remember it was a quick decision, within a few weeks of the start of production.

When you got the part of Lewis, did you know from the start, that you would film five episodes?
No, the part called for one episode (possibly two) as I recall, and I was then written into further episodes. I recall that episodes would be written a few weeks ahead of shooting. Can this really be true?

Was there any mention of bringing your character back for series two and three?
That was not mentioned at the time I was filming. I remember I was sad that I was leaving the friendly and close crew after completion of my episodes. I also remember that I was something of a challenging youth at the time, and wonder if I was too much to handle (my projection at the time perhaps).

Christian Rodska (Ron), Paul Guess (Lewis Hammond) and Arthur English (Slugger) in a scene from Steve

Paul Guess as Lewis Hammond

Christian Rodska (Ron) and Paul Guess (Lewis Hammond)

You had quite a few horse and motor bike riding scenes for the show – could you ride before being cast as Lewis?
Yes I had ridden horses several years before for a 6 week TV series 'The New Forest Rustlers' for Southern Television. I think that I fitted the bill for the part, as I was willing and able to both ride a motor bike and a horse at the time.

Has any particular episode or scene remained in your memory?
I remember well the scene in which the nightriders stormed the stable yard and released a number of horses from their stalls. It was a challenging setup calling for the riders to open a series of latches on the stall doors from horseback, while causing a state of panic so that the horses would stampede from the stable yard (we had already opened the yard gate by bending down from the horses on the way in).

That scene was clearly dangerous for the actors, and perhaps with hindsight potentially traumatic and dangerous for the horses. Fortunately it went with great precision and no damage was done.

Looking back on the episode I see that it worked very well, and I doubt that a scene could be shot for TV in the same way today.

Looking back I recall the Follyfoot episodes with fondness. We spent countless hours out of doors on the farm, and at various locations around Yorkshire. At the time I was very new to the country life, and wonder if this time endeared me to the country living that I now enjoy so much.

Episode 3: Gypsy

Directed by Ian McFarlane

The Story

The Colonel and Dora are looking after a gypsy pony which has been badly treated by two brothers, Amos and Reuben, who believe that a gypsy's curse caused one of them to have a serious riding accident. The gypsy was riding across their land when the brothers attacked his pony; the gypsy fought back with a knife and was arrested and put in jail. Released from jail the gypsy tells the Colonel he wants revenge. Stryker warns the two brothers. Amos rides to Follyfoot and threatens to kill the gypsy if he goes on their land again.

Amos frightens the pony which Dora is holding. Dora lets go and the pony runs off to Kellett's farm where the brothers lock him in the barn. Steve plans a rescue with the gypsy who gets the pony out, but Steve notices another horse and gets locked in the barn. Pretending to be a gypsy Steve threatens to curse the brothers again if they do not let him out with the horse. Dora arrives, nearly making a mess of things by saying Steve is not a Gypsy, but Reuben has had enough and when Steve says that if they get rid of the horse their luck may change, he is allowed to take the horse home to add to Dora's collection.

Tommy Boyle (Gypsy), Walter Sparrow (Amos Kellett) and Gillian Blake (Dora)

My Story

Gypsy took me back in time because the location, which was at Shadwell and belonged to Mr Cyril Townend (Squib for short), was where I got my first pony – Danny Boy (or Hit and Miss when we were show jumping, because he either stopped at the fence or knocked it down). I kept my pony there for about three years and it felt good that this location would be used for filming *Follyfoot*, more than once.

Cyril was a real character and Tony Essex liked him so much he based the two brothers on him. He also wanted to include him in a shot, but for some reason this was never shown. The pony we used was from Cyril's stables so he knew his way around, which made it easier to make him run into the yard and into the barn. To make the pony look nervous the horse girl was out of shot with the lunge whip, making it scrape along the ground so the pony would jump around wondering what the noise was. We could not make too much noise otherwise the sound boom would pick it up and the sound would have to be dubbed over. Sadly this happened quite a lot!

When Steve was in the barn with the 'cursed' horse, I noticed how naturally he interacted with it when feeding him with the famous horse nuts that were always on standby. Steve said later it was not instinctive, he had learned it from watching the Horse Girls.

Tommy Boyle in an unused scene from **Gypsy**

Episode 4: Shadow

Directed by Frederic Goode

The Story

Shadow, a very valuable horse belonging to the Squire and ridden by his daughter Isabel (Virginia Denham) is seen for the first time by Steve and Dora out hunting. Shadow stops at a hedge and throws Isabel off. Dora and the Colonel go to the Squire's to watch Isabel taking Shadow over some show jumps, when again he stops. Dora takes Shadow back to Follyfoot to give him some schooling, using kindness and not the whip.

Ron needs some money to mend his bike, which has broken down when riding with his friend Lewis. He sees a way of making money by taking the now re-schooled and jumping Shadow, to the point-to-point and places bets on him to win. To get Shadow away from Follyfoot, Lewis rings the Colonel and pretends to be the Squire's groom, saying the Squire will pick up the horse later that day. Ron rides Shadow in the race but sadly Shadow stops. All the bets are lost and Ron is in trouble again. Dora rides Shadow home and jumps every fence in sight.

Billy Bland (Shadow) arriving at Follyfoot Farm

My Story

The horse that played Shadow was called Billy Bland and belonged to Major Birtwhistle, an acquaintance of mine who owned Harrogate Equestrian Centre. Billy was an old favourite of his and one which had competed in Three Day Events. I felt quite privileged that I was allowed to take him to Follyfoot for filming.

It was quite useful that Billy had a bit of 'knapp' in him, which meant he did not always do as we wanted or go where we wanted, which proved an asset with the jumping. For many of the jumping scenes we used stunt rider Sadie Eddon and she did get him jumping quite well. Eagle-eyed viewers may have spotted my hand holding Shadow's bridle when Isabel returns to the horse after her fall whilst hunting.

The Point-to-Point was held on the old Bramham Moor course near Harewood. Some of the shooting was taken on the actual day, but the section of the race scene where Shadow stops, was shot another day with a few extras riding racehorses and Roy Alon doing the stunt riding for Ron on Shadow. This proved interesting. Roy was mounted on Shadow and he was told to make him stop at the fence. He had never ridden at a fence before and when it was time for the take, the horse jumped the fence like a true professional. All Roy could say was, 'Wow! That was great'. For some reason we could not get Shadow to stop clearing the fence, so we had to swap to one of the other horses which could be made to stop.

The Squire (William Mervyn) riding Forrester

Filming the hunt scene from Shadow

Episode 5: One White-Foot Charley

Directed by Ian McFarlane

The Story

Charley, said to be the oldest pit pony in the world, is retired to Follyfoot. Ex-miner Tom (Bert Palmer) often thinks of his old pit pony Jacky, and when his son offers to take him to see his old pit, Tom says how much he would like to see Jacky again and wonders if maybe they could find him.

At Follyfoot, Dora and Steve are out riding and see the Night Riders and Lewis. Steve tackles Lewis, who lashes out with his whip and causes Steve's horse to rear and throw him off. Lewis's horse is also lame; Dora and Steve decide they want to do something about it. Dora swaps clothes with Callie (Gillian Bailey) and goes to Hammonds to hire the lame horse so they can get the vet out to look at it. The Colonel is not supposed to know, but arrives with the vet who sees Charley laid out and suggests he should be put down the next day.

Tom and his son eventually trace Jacky to Follyfoot and see Charley who recognises his handler from the past, but they are told Charley is near the end of his life. Dora introduces him to Folly the foal. 'See 'em come see 'em go, that's how it should be', Tom says.

Lewis brings the lame horse to be cared for at Follyfoot until he is better.

Christopher Coll (George Platt) and Bert Palmer (Tom Platt) with Jacky

My Story

Charley was an old pony with a docked tail, who had never been down a pit in his life. He came from stables at Headingley, owned by a local celebrity known as the 'Headingly Cowboy', who was regularly to be seen on local TV and riding his western horse through the streets of Leeds. I had the chance to ride the horse and was told not to pull on his reins as he would go faster rather than slow down, but if I said the word 'whoa' he would stop dead in his tracks. I found this to be true, the hard way!

For the scene where the Vet thought Charley had died, one of the stunt riders taught him to lie down. This did not take much doing. Charley seemed quite grateful for the help and the rest. There was no problem in getting him to move his ear to show the Vet he was still alive – it just happened. Charley was quite happy just to lie there and when we shouted at him to get up, all he moved was his ear!

The stuntman who rode for Steve did not really have to do much because Forrester would rear quite naturally, and usually did so when we least expected it. For his part of the stunt, Steve just rolled himself off the back of a low truck!

Charley was a bit on the thin side when he arrived to film, but when the owner collected him some weeks later he was delighted with his improved condition.

Episode 6: The Charity Horse

Directed by Stephen Frears

The Story

Gip (Bryan Sweeney) has a pony called Sandy. Gip's older brother Willy (Len Jones) takes Sandy out with his late father's cart to sell firewood. A newspaper reporter wants to write an article about him and put his picture in the local paper.

The pony is frightened by the camera flash and bolts into the path of an oncoming wagon and is killed. In the meantime Gip and his mother (Margery Mason), not knowing about the accident, come to Follyfoot Farm to see if Sandy can retire there. Ron Stryker tells Gip all the horses are badly treated and unhappy.

The newspaper runs a charity appeal to buy a pony to replace Sandy; the one they buy is not fit to work. Gip wants to keep it, but after seeing his mother crying because they cannot afford to keep a non-working pony, he decides to take it to Follyfoot Farm. Stryker causes more trouble by frightening the charity pony with his motorbike; the pony bolts, Gip falls off and rolls down into a quarry.

The pony saves Gip's life by staying at the top of the quarry and showing where Gip has fallen. Gip is allowed to keep the pony and the Newspaper has another heartwarming story to tell.

My Story

In this episode we decided to get Steve a horse which he would find easier to ride, so I went to see Cyril Townend. We had used his stables for a location in Episode 3 *Gypsy*.

I asked if he had any horses for sale. It was not often he had because he loved them too much. He showed me Alex, who had nearly died with anaemia. He would let us buy him as long as we did not work him too hard and had him checked out by the vet. This was no problem as all the horses were checked out each year before filming to make sure they could do the work we wanted. YTV bought Alex, who arrived at Follyfoot and became the main horse Steve rode for the rest of the series. The only real problem we ever had with Alex was his aversion to pigs!

The pony who took the part of old Sandy had not been in harness for a long time, and the first time we tried him he kicked out and broke the shafts of the cart. This was the time to call for specialist help, so I got in touch with Donald Hardy. He had a team of coach horses and was very knowledgeable in the art of driving horses. He came to Follyfoot and told us it was all *our* fault. The shafts on the cart were much too long so he shortened them and hey presto, the pony did not put a foot wrong.

We had to make it appear that Sandy, pulling the cart, was bolting down the street in Wetherby without a driver. When it came to filming we had a stuntman hidden under a blanket on the cart to do the actual driving.

Bryan Sweeney (Gip) sitting on the wood cart

He had just a little space to look through in order to see where he was going – rather him than me!

Kip, the pony used in the swimming scene in Episode 2 *Steve*, also appeared in this episode. All he was required to do was to jump a little log. We knew he would not do it because of his foot problem but his owner had taught him to do little rears. This was useful because it made him look naughty and as if he was refusing to jump. Eventually Dora led Kip over the log. When she re-mounted him she had to turn his head sharply round, or he would have walked off set and straight into the camera.

I recently spoke to Gillian Croft, one of the Horse Girls, who had got in touch with me following my interview for Radio Leeds. She told me that the charity pony misbehaved whilst the presentation ceremony was being filmed. Much to her embarrassment he had dragged her down the street in front of all the cast and crew.

Episode 7: Know-All's-Nag

Directed by Stephen Frears

The Story

Gip is looking after Marty, the Charity Horse, who keeps getting out of his stable. Out riding, Steve and Dora find Marty and return him to Gip. Steve is shocked at how the horse is being looked after. Gip tells Steve that someone keeps letting Marty out of his stable. Steve and Gip hide in the stable loft and discover the culprit is Willy, Gip's brother.

Gip runs off with Marty and Steve finds him at a disused railway station. He sees that the horse has colic because he had been given cold water when he was too hot.

Steve comes to the rescue, gets the horse up and gives it a drench (a liquid remedy for horse colic). Marty recovers and they return to Follyfoot where Marty is to remain.

My Story

In this episode Marty had to act as though he had colic. It was suggested we put an irritant on the horse to make him kick his stomach. We Horse Girls were up in arms at this suggestion and stood round the horse to prevent it from happening. Because we felt so strongly about this, it was decided to go to the expense of getting a horse which was fully trained by circus animal trainer Mary Chipperfield. The horse was beautiful, and we all fell in love with him, but he had a sad story. When the circus was touring, someone had set fire to where the horses were kept, some were killed or had to be put down. Fortunately this talented horse was saved, but was badly scarred from burns he had received.

In the colic scene the horse performed brilliantly, but times have changed and colic is now treated with drugs rather than a drench.

Gip with the Charity Horse

Episode 8: Moonstone

Directed by Michael Apted

The Story

Callie is at the circus with her mother where they see Moonstone, whom Callie thinks is being mistreated and needs to be rescued. She tries to persuade the Colonel to buy the horse but he refuses. In the middle of a stormy night Callie steals Moonstone from the Circus and takes him to Follyfoot Farm where she asks Steve to help her hide him. Steve unwillingly suggests she takes Moonstone to the shed by the lake and give him some hay. Moonstone's owner from the circus arrives to be told her horse has not been seen.

The police become involved and come to Follyfoot Farm to look for Moonstone. Callie is seen going to the shed to feed the horse.

Callie's mother persuades the Colonel to buy Moonstone. Steve is sent with the cash to find the Circus and buy the horse. The police return to Follyfoot and discover the horse, but by then Steve has done the deal and Moonstone belongs to the Colonel.

Moonstone performing

My Story

This episode was all filmed at Follyfoot Farm. The Circus set was built by the side of the farmhouse and the night shoots really took place at night and the rain was produced by the fire brigade. Alex doubled for the Circus horse in the rain scenes, as the circus horse owner did not want their horse getting wet because they could not risk him catching cold.

I was told that it was this particular episode which won us the 1971 BAFTA Harlequin Award for the best children's TV programme.

I remember another personal story from when we were filming this episode. All of the Horse Girls worked seven days a week during filming, but as Horse Manager I was working on the day shoots as well as supervising the night shoots. I became totally exhausted and extremely bad tempered. The Horse Girls knew it was best to keep out of my way, but the production manager found me crying in the top barn (which I always did when I was over tired). He asked what was wrong. He really had no idea what to do with me, so he rang Tony Essex whose solution was to send a black taxi with a bottle of gin for me on the back seat. I sobbed, 'What good is that going to do', and continued my crying. Tony was got in touch with again and another black taxi arrived. This time the back seat contained Tony himself. 'What is wrong girl?' he demanded. I said I was exhausted and fed up. He replied, 'Do you think a pay rise would help?' 'No,' I said, 'I just need some sleep and some time off'.

He said I could have a day off but only as long as everything was left OK for filming and the Horse Girls could manage. I remember thinking 'thanks for nothing'. It was very good of him to take time out to visit the set and try to solve my problem, but he really could not understand what was wrong. (Nor did I get the pay rise!)

Follyfoot and the circus

In Conversation with Gillian Bush-Bailey (Callie Holmes)

GILLIAN APPEARED IN THE FOLLOWING EPISODES:

Series 1:

STEVE
Directed by Frederick Goode

ONE WHITE FOOT CHARLEY
Directed by Ian McFarlane

MOONSTONE
Directed by Michael Apted

Series 2:

OUT OF THE BLUE HORSE
Directed by Peter Hammond

How did you get the part of Callie in Follyfoot?
I can't remember. I was doing quite a lot of work at the time and I guess I was asked to go for an interview.

Could you already ride a horse, or did you have to learn for the part?
Riding – a thorny subject! My sister had a horse, and being six years younger and refusing to do anything my big sister did – I chose Ballet and Tap – and refused to go near the horse! He was big though (fourteen hands part Arab gelding – who liked the sound of the hunting horn…terrifying) and I was quite a small youngster. So I could sit on a horse OK and be led round looking like I had a reasonable 'seat' – but I went for lessons with a lady outside Windsor, who worked with actors, and knew the kind of things I needed to be ok about. The problem was that her horses were trained – I don't think the Follyfoot horses had ever seen a light or camera, let alone a mark on the ground that they had to stop on for the shot – so they didn't much like it. The pony I rode was intent upon biting my bottom if he got half a chance, and once bolted across the field with me. I still remember my mum being there shouting, 'turn it, turn it' . I just hung on – would have been best if I fell off I guess – got it over and done with – but I never did.

Were you on set with Robin Stewart at all, who was originally cast to play Paul, before being replaced by Steve Hodson?
Yes, I think we shot part of the first episode – but I don't remember much about him I'm afraid.

Can you describe a typical day on set at Hollin Hall?
Cold…..cold and wet. Getting on set early…going into the farmhouse we used for makeup and costume – then we had a caravan I think, but that might be second series. Having bacon butties from the catering van – tea and coffee – waiting round in the COLD. Trying to rehearse with the animals…trying to remember what the animals were meant to do and get the lines right and what we had to do…again and again…and it was so COLD!

When you got the part, did you know at that time, how many episodes you would appear in?
No – I remember not wanting to do the second series – you may have realised by now this was not a happy job for me! But they said something about plans for a film, and I needed to do an episode from the second series called *Out of the Blue Horse*, if I wanted to do the film – which I would have liked to do.

Did you personally get much response from fans of the show?
Not really – Double Deckers is the

one people tend to remember. Some do mention Follyfoot – usually the episode where I rode in to the yard in hot pants ….was it cold that day!

Where did you stay whilst making the series?
In a B&B in Leeds – rather bleak actually – but there was lovely lady in costume who took me in to her home for the odd tea after filming.

Why do you think the series has become a cult classic?
Horses I think – every girl's dream? Well some girls!

Tony Essex was Executive producer and scriptwriter – how would you describe him?
The only thing I remember is meeting him in the studios before we went to the farm for the first shooting – he said to me 'I hope you can bloody well ride' – hmmmmm.

Did you watch the daily rushes after filming? Did you manage to see any of the series when it was shown, and have you seen any of the newly released DVD's?
No – didn't see rushes, saw some of the series – didn't know about the DVD but have seen a bit of an episode on You Tube.

Has any particular episode or scene remained in your memory?
Moonstone I guess – I have a memory that Gillian Blake was away for a few days so I got to do pretty well most of the episode – not sure it was written to be 'Callie's episode' – but it turned out that way I think.

There were several directors who have gone on to be very top names including Michael Apted and Peter Hammond – did you have a favourite director?
Michael Apted – he directed Moonstone and it was he who told me about the award the series got – 1972 Best Children's Drama – no one else did – I bumped into him in a lift in the BBC TV centre and he asked me if I knew.

Any memories of working with Desmond Llewelyn and Arthur English?
Arthur was a delight – this is one of those I wish I knew then what I know now moments….I would like to talk to him more about the end of the music halls – his wide-boy act – his extraordinary long and successful career in a kind of theatre, that doesn't really exist anymore. Christian Rodska and I worked together after Follyfoot – on Eagle of the Ninth, a BBC serial.

I also remember one moment of fun – although very unprofessional – might have been in Moonstone – Gillian and I had a scene with Desmond – we had to go into his study very shamefaced and get a ticking off – it was just before lunch break and Gillian had a huge stomach rumble (I don't think it was mine), that sent us into peals of laughter – once done – we couldn't stop! They were keen to get this shot done and then strike to another location for filming after lunch – but we couldn't stop corpsing – I don't think we needed any more stomach rumbles – we just kept laughing…. and having to do endless takes – I can't remember whether we managed to do it before lunch break or not! Terrible behaviour!

Did you ever revisit the farm after the series ended?
No! It really wasn't a happy job for me – I always felt on the edge of the show really – I don't recall ever being invited to a wrap party (end of shoot do) or, as I said above – even being told when the show did well – I certainly didn't see or hear from any of the cast outside being on set. I was younger than the other actors of course, fifteen or sixteen on the first series and I remember having a very miserable seventeenth birthday while filming – the last time I went there – June 1972 I guess.

Episode 9: Stryker's Good Deed

Directed by Maurice Hatton

The Story

For once, Ron attempts a good deed and helps Jon Jon, a horse whose owner, a Rag and Bone man, has been taken ill. It is suggested that the horse is put down, but Ron decides to take it to Follyfoot Farm for Gip to look after until the owner recovers. Jon Jon escapes from Follyfoot and Dora rides after him on Dancer, a horse which the Colonel has told her not to ride. She has an accident.

Gip visits the Rag and Bone man in hospital and learns that Jon Jon will always run home if he gets the chance. Gip finds the horse and stays to look after him at the Rag and Bone man's yard. Steve finds them and insists Jon Jon goes with him back to Follyfoot. Ron lets Jon Jon out of his stable, and the horse goes home where Gip can look after him.

My Story

Jon Jon was a genuine Rag and Bone pony found by one of the Horse Girls. He had really had a hard life and he had scars on his body from a badly-fitting harness, he was also quite thin and looked very sad. At Follyfoot fiction sometimes became a reality. For the storylines we often had to find horses which looked the part of an ill-treated animal. We were delighted on the occasions we were able to return them to their owners looking better than when they came.

When Dora falls off Dancer it was once again Sadie Eddon, the stunt rider, who doubled. There was also a double for Steve. By now both Gillian and Steve were competent riders but for safety and insurance reasons they could not do their own stunts. I was asked by Tony Essex to do a press interview on filming with the horses. I really got a telling off from him for letting the stunt double information out to the press; to me it was just telling the truth.

Ron did not use a stunt double for the difficult task of leading Jon Jon whilst riding his motor bike.

If you manage to watch the episode on DVD you may notice right at the end, Jon Jon is actually running back to Follyfoot Farm. Maybe he thought it was better than home!

Ron on his bike

Episode 10: Mr. She-Knows

Directed by Vic Hughes

The Story

A lonely old man has no one but his old horse, Gloria, who is retired at Follyfoot Farm. Dora finds that Gloria is missing from her stable and discovers her in the field with the old man. She is not pleased and tells the Colonel, who instructs her to leave them alone.

In the evening, Gloria is brought back into her stable followed by the old man, Mr Mallet (Richard Goolden). The Colonel gives permission for him to stay in the stable with Gloria overnight and tells Ron to take some food out to him. Ron taunts the old man and chucks the food on the roof of the stables. Ron is leaving to go home when he revs his bike and makes one of the horses in the stables jump and knock the lantern over, causing a fire. Dora, Steve and Slugger manage to put the fire out without anyone or the horses getting hurt. To prevent Ron being sacked his father pays for the damage and for Gloria to go back home with Mr Mallet.

Fire scene in the stable

My Story

I must admit that when I read the fire scene in the script it did worry me. However, we were told it would be safe and the horses would not get hurt. When it came to shooting the scene, a brown sticky substance was painted on the doors and stable side walls where the flames were to be seen. When lit, only the sticky substance burned and none of the woodwork was damaged.

Part of the rescue scene, where only a smoke effect was used, had two horses with a Horse Girl behind each to shoo them out when Slugger opened the doors.

During the main burning sequence and the rescue of the old man, Gloria was not in her stall, but was then put back for the shot to show her being saved. As a reward, Gloria was given a drink of orange juice as it was a favourite of hers.

We selected three horses with placid temperaments and used them in the burning stables sequences. They were amazingly good and did not seem worried by the flames. I wondered if they would go back in after the fire but there was no problem with any of them, perhaps because there was no lingering smell of fire from the material used.

It turned out that we Horse Girls had been the most scared.

Gloria enjoys her orange juice

Follyfoot Remembered: Hazel Cleasson

CONTINUITY ON THE FOLLOWING EPISODES:

Series 1:

STEVE
GYPSY
SHADOW
MOONSTONE
MR. SHE-KNOWS
THE STANDSTILL HORSE

Series 2:

TREASURE HUNT

I was involved with seven episodes… felt it was less. The two things that immediately come into my memory are the 'lightning tree', and the *Mr She Knows* episode.

The old tree (oak I think) had been lifted and put into the ground surrounded by concrete. Officially dead – but when spring came there was still enough sap in the tree for it to start to bud and then leaf. The chore of 'de-leafing' the unfortunate tree was given over to props – for obvious reasons! If I remember rightly, they were not best pleased. The other one was related to the *Mr. She-Knows* episode, when Jane Royston, Horse Manager, initially chose a stallion instead of a mare for the lead role – maybe she will have some memories herself regarding that!

When Follyfoot was being shot I was but a freshly trained P.A./Continuity Girl. I knew what was expected but theory and fact, as I discovered very quickly, are not the same thing. As far as costume and makeup were concerned, I liaised closely with makeup

Christian Rodska (Ron) filming for the episode **Steve**

Desmond Llewelyn (Colonel) and Richard Goolden (Mr Mallet) in between scenes for **Mr. She-Knows**

and wardrobe. If I did not have a good Polaroid of any artiste, I would cross reference with them, and vice versa.

The whole series was on film, so it was not possible to ask for a playback to check anything – YOU (i.e. continuity) had to get it right. Mistakes could be costly. If there was a need to reshoot or do pick-up shots, then these notes were vital. Apart from the action continuity notes we would also log the lens, T-stop, lighting etc so that the whole ambiance could be re-created as closely as possible to the original set up. When rushes were seen in the evening I would take the opportunity of checking my notes with what was on the screen, just to set my mind at rest.

When I first started on location I was a fairly slim, if not to say skinny, individual. But with a diet of three breakfasts things changed. Breakfast number one was when I got up; Mike Donnelly, sound man, would pick me up from my home and we would then rendezvous with the crew at the YTV canteen for breakfast number two. Breakfast number three was on site where location caterers were serving (yes you're right) a brilliant cooked breakfast. Location lunch was three courses, plus afternoon tea with fresh cream cakes etc.

If there was a night shoot, then the location caterer's homemade soups, pies and meals were to die for. It sounds as if we staggered from one meal to the next; not the case. The days were long and hard and we were often in the back of beyond and in very cold conditions, so I feel we tended to burn it off!

On very cold, windy night shoots, the most favourite place to stand was near the Arc Light condensers – the warmest place to be when waiting for the set to be dressed, or for artistes to rehearse before committing to celluloid.

I thoroughly enjoyed the time I spent with both the cast and crew. A bit like being part of an extended family that lives, laughs and argues with each other, but without malice. And, if called upon, would help you out no matter what.

I do remember Anne Ayoub – she was responsible for continuity on seventeen Follyfoot episodes. She used to terrify me because she exuded so much confidence and skill, but she always meant well. She did not suffer fools, but if you asked her something she would tell you. She could be a hard task mistress, but it was worth it.

Episode 11: The Standstill Horse

Directed by Ian McFarlane

The Story

The Night Riders are in action again, this time chasing Ginny (Petra Markham), a disabled girl out riding. Steve and Dora come to the rescue but are accidentally overheard by one of the Night Riders saying where Ginny lives. The Night Riders go to Ginny's at night and chase her pony, Clipper, who tries to jump over the fence and is killed.

Steve and Dora decide to help by replacing Clipper. They build a special platform and train one of their ponies to stand still long enough for Ginny to mount it. Ginny's father does not want her to have another pony and returns it to Follyfoot. However, when he sees a little boy who is scared of horses, successfully ride the pony, he is persuaded by the Colonel to let his daughter keep it.

My Story

Clipper came from a riding school for the disabled in Horsforth (Leeds) and was fully trained. But we needed another pony to be trained up as Clipper's replacement. She was actually trained by the Horse Girls with much help from Gillian. Plenty of patience and treats were required as we went along filming scene by scene. By the end she would stand at the platform exactly as required.

The opening chase scene was staged by Peter Diamond and the same stunt riders were used as in the first two episodes. Sadie Eddon's daughter doubled for Ginny and one of the Horse Girls doubled for Steve. On the bikes Lewis (Paul Guess) did his own stunts, as he had done in previous episodes.

Petra Markham (Ginny Tuckwood) in **The Standstill Horse**

Episode 12: Birthday at Follyfoot

Directed by Michael Tuchner

The Story

Dora is hoping to keep her approaching birthday secret but does not realise that Ron has found out. He tries to discover what Dora would like if she could have anything she wanted. Steve also knows it is Dora's birthday and this causes a competition between the two boys that ends up with them jousting; the winner can decide how to celebrate the birthday. Neither of them knows that Slugger has already got it planned.

In the end Steve provides a cake, Ron provides the champagne and Slugger organises the boys to build a raft so Dora can celebrate on the lake.

The most important present is from her Uncle. It is Copper, a beautiful chestnut Welsh-Arab cross, with four white legs and flaxen mane and tail.

Filming the waterborne birthday party

My Story

The jousting scene took place in Harewood Park and was again arranged by Peter Diamond using horses from Reg Dent, a well respected supplier of horses to the film world. The fairground used for the location of the jousting was setting up for a Bank Holiday Weekend event at Harewood, but the jousting was specially staged for the filming.

Dora was always seen riding different horses in the series so I suggested to Tony Essex that she should actually have one special horse of her own. Tony thought this was a great idea as it also solved a problem which had existed since early in the series. Flash was Dora's horse early on, but could not be kept for the whole series as her owner, Countess Wenckheim, required her to go to stud! This led to the episode written about Dora's birthday, as being the ideal opportunity to provide her with her own horse, for future series.

Copper was bought from Mount Pleasant Stud (Scarcroft, Leeds) as a three-year-old and only just broken in. He did not like standing still very much and quickly got impatient. Gillian and he gradually grew together, gaining trust and developing a partnership – he really was a great little horse.

It was not too long before Tony gave Copper to Gillian as a present and she kept him for all of his life.

Gillian Blake on Copper Prince

***The cast in a scene from* Birthday at Follyfoot**

Follyfoot Remembered: Allan Pyrah

Camera Assistant

I joined Yorkshire Television from a small local film company called Five City Films based in Bradford, in June 1968. The studios weren't built at that time, but fortunately there was an empty trouser factory across the road, which is where YTV first operated from, stockpiling programmes for when it went on air. Peter Jackson had joined earlier in the year to set up the fledgling film department. I worked with Frank Pocklington and Peter until approximately 1975 when I started doing my own documentaries and dramas.

I'm not sure, but I think that I worked on the whole series as camera assistant, which in those days meant doing the clapperboard and focus pulling. In later years when the workload became too heavy, we managed to get an operator on board.

I do remember that it was a happy time – we used to play football at lunchtime. Mike Tuchner (the director) played like a Whirling Dervish. Not sure if that's how you spell that!

Then there was the pub run – a mini-van full of sparks, camera crew, directors etc – speeding up to the *Harewood Arms* for a quick pint or two, and then back at twice the speed to grab anything that was left from the caterers.

There was an occasion when someone decided that it was time to have a union card check. An elderly camera operator called Eric Besch was the focus of the union rep's attention, and he approached Eric and asked to see proof that he was a fully paid-up member. Eric slowly got out his card and showed the rep his number, which if I can remember was under 30, a founder member!

The other thing I remember is the black taxi – whenever we saw it coming down the track we knew someone was in trouble – it was Tony Essex (head of drama I think at the time). I also remember we had an American director once who dressed all in white – I think he only lasted two days!

A rare picture of Ron Stryker on a different kind of horse power!

Episode 13: A Day in the Sun

Directed by Mike Purcell

The Story

Steve sees a newspaper article about his mother who is in trouble near Liverpool. Searching for his mother, he hears about a horse that has been very badly treated and asks the Colonel for help. He is told he cannot take the horse but stubbornly says he is not coming back without it. The horse arrives at Follyfoot near to death and should be put down, but Steve wants to give it, a day in the sun. Steve associates the horse's situation with that of his mother and confides in Dora who has just come back from a dance with Ron.

The horse is put down and Steve goes to Liverpool to find his mother. Dora feels that things at Follyfoot will never be the same again, even though Steve says he will be back.

My Story

This was the final episode of the first series and written to provide a strong follow-on for the already commissioned series two.

It was not particularly heavy on horse action.

From the outset all the stables at Follyfoot were designed so partitions could be taken out in order to provide room to film horses lying down and accommodate the actors, lights, cameras and the rest of the crew. For the sick horse we used a heavily made up, but otherwise very healthy, stunt horse.

Clare Kelly (Kathy Ross) – Steve's mother

Moving to Winter Quarters

Filming for the first series had now finished and it was time to close Follyfoot Farm down and to take the horses to their winter quarters, which were at Janet Harrison's parents' farm on the Harrogate Road.

The older horses were kept out during the day and brought in to stables at night. The main horses, such as Alex, Sirocco and Sky, were all clipped out and kept in work and occasionally taken to the local shows for the Show Jumping. A couple of the Horse Girls and I were paid to look after the horses even though we were not filming, and it was quite nice just to have the horses to ourselves. Copper, who had been given to Gillian, was taken south to Sadie Eddon's yard in Windsor so Gillian could still ride him. I must say I missed him as he had lots of character and was also a good show jumper, so he would have done well at the shows.

When it was time to commence filming for the second series, Tony Essex got in touch with me about the new scripts, and which horses we would need and what he hoped we could get them to do. This also gave us time to get Follyfoot Farm up and running again, although it was about April time and it was still quite cold and the weather could be very bleak.

Our living quarters had originally been in the house. It consisted of one bedroom in which three of us had to sleep and a kitchen and a toilet, which was downstairs. You could say it really was not ideal, especially as there was no bathroom. Yorkshire Television provided transport to take us to and from the Studios where we could get a shower and also end the night in the Television Bar where you never knew whom you would meet. Diana Dors, Gerald Harper, Les Dawson, Hughie Green and Alan Whicker, just to mention a few.

For Series Two guess what? We were to move out of the house into a mobile home, which was much better in every way. A unit was also provided with showers and toilets, but we still went to the Studios most nights; it was much more fun!

I must say the mobile home was a great improvement as we always had somewhere to go out of the cold. The electric fire was on all the time unless the weather was very warm. The house now had more sets put in and was only used for filming. Not just for Follyfoot but also for interior shots that were meant to be elsewhere.

In Conversation with Christian Rodska (Ron Stryker)

Where did you audition for the role and what did that consist of?
I did a film test at Hollin Hall (Follyfoot Farm), riding my 1958 Triumph Tiger Cub motor bike to the audition. I was asked if I could ride a horse, and I said yes – which was a little white lie. When I discovered I had got the role of Ron Stryker I took some riding lessons. As well as getting the part, the producer also liked my bike, and it was especially written into the series for me.

Did you have an outline of the character?
Ron Stryker was based on a character in the book Cobbler's Dream, and was quite a nasty individual. When Monica Dickens, who wrote the book, visited the Follyfoot set, she gave me a signed copy and she wrote in it, 'Stryker was never half as lovable a rogue as you make him – I hope you go on having fun, Monica Dickens'.

Describe a typical day on the set.
If we were filming at the farm I would arrive around 7.30am and go into wardrobe and make-up. We would be handed any rewrites, and then start filming. We broke for lunch around 1pm and usually had a game of football or cricket with the crew. We would film some more scenes in the afternoon, usually finishing around 5.30pm depending on the time of year. Sometimes we would

Christian Rodska (Ron) in a scene from **Mr She Knows**

stay on later if the director wanted a particular lighting effect. Each episode took around 7-10 days to shoot, and they would aim to get around three minutes of film per day. The series would usually begin transmission whilst we were still filming the later episodes.

When you got the role of Ron Stryker, did you know at the time the series would run for thirty-nine episodes?
No, I originally signed for one series, but towards the end of the first run they realised how popular the show had become and I signed for the second series, with an option for a third.

Tony Essex (Executive Producer) and author Monica Dickens

Christian Rodska (Ron) and Gillian Blake (Dora) in between filming Four Legged Hat

Does any particular episode remain in your memory?
I remember filming one called Mr She Knows, *from the first series. The storyline revolved around a mysterious old gentleman hanging around the stables, which was really upsetting Dora. The Colonel took pity on him, and let him stay overnight in the stable – suggesting to Slugger that he took him some of the infamous stew! This gave Ron an idea of how to get rid of the old man, and he volunteered to take the*

Christian Rodska on his infamous motor bike

Christian Rodska (Ron)

Follyfoot was sold to over twenty countries – what response was there from overseas?
I know the series was very popular in Germany, Australia and New Zealand.

When you were nearing the end of the third series was there any mention of a fourth?
Not a fourth series, but all the actors were retained to do a Follyfoot film, to be directed by David Hemmings. At the time a lot of other television series were doing feature length film spin-offs, and as far as I know the film script was written.

Did you ever revisit the farm location after the series ended?
Not that I can remember. When I wasn't filming, I used to take my wife and young son, Ben, up there at the weekends to have a picnic by the lake. We often met some of the directors and crew, who were busy planning the filming of the next episode.

Follyfoot won the 1972 Best Children's Drama Award from the Society of Film and Television Arts – why do you think the series was so successful?
It had the coveted Sunday teatime slot, and it was pure family viewing. It had very high production values; it was all shot on film, and had Tony Essex as its brilliant executive producer.

You lived in Yorkshire whilst filming Follyfoot – how long after the series did you continue living there?
I guess I must have stayed for another four or five years. I worked on shows such as In Loving Memory and This Year, Next Year, which were both filmed in Yorkshire.

meal out to him. Just as the old man was about to take the welcome meal, Ron pulled the plate away from him and threw it away, up over the stable roof. In Ron's mind, without food, the old man would soon be on his way and life at Follyfoot could return to normal. I did think Ron was particularly nasty in that scene, and the only way I could justify it was that Ron would do anything for Dora, and he could see how upset she was about the unwelcome guest.

In the same episode, I remember I had a scene repairing the roof of the donkey pen. In the script I had to come down a ladder from the roof, and for a laugh I thought I would do it the way that you sometimes see in comedy films. I put one foot either side of the ladder and slid all the way down to the bottom.

Unfortunately, I landed badly, went over on my ankle, and it immediately swelled up. Nursing a bad sprain, I then had to go back up the ladder again and reshoot the scene!

Whose idea was it to continually smash your bike through the Follyfoot gate?
I had just started work on the first series, and the director came up to me, and asked, 'How would Ron Stryker approach the closed Follyfoot Farm gate?' I went and got my bike, started it up and rode straight at the gate – having made sure it was off the latch beforehand! It was my idea, and mine alone, and was used frequently. I also did all my own bike riding sequences throughout the series.

What became of your infamous motor-bike – registration 510 CAC?
Unfortunately a few years ago, I made the classic mistake of stripping it down completely to re-build it, and sent a couple of parts away to be re-sprayed and re-chromed, and they never came back to me. All the other parts of the machine are in boxes in my garage, but I do hope to get it running again one day.

49

Christian Rodska (Ron)

Did you have a favourite director?
Follyfoot had several distinguished directors and I enjoyed working with them all, as they each bought their own unique quality to the show. I particularly enjoyed working with Jack Cardiff, Desmond Davis and Gareth Davies, and kept in touch with them over the years.

Away from acting what do you like doing in your free time?
I really enjoy sailing, and I have my own boat. I am also a qualified pilot, and own a microlite.

Some time ago, there was talk of remaking the series – could it be remade?
Yes it could, but you would lose the innocence – children today are a lot more streetwise, and that would need to be reflected in the story line.

You mentioned Tony Essex – how much time did he usually spend on the set?
At odd times during the filming Tony would appear. We would usually see this black taxi cab trundling down the track to Hollin Hall, and everyone would be on their best behaviour!

Did you watch the daily rushes after filming?
Yes, I liked to see them because I could watch and, hopefully, learn from them.

What reaction did you get from the fans?
A lot of people would recognise me from the series, and would come up and have a chat. I still receive fan mail, and get recognised – usually by the parents whose children are now watching the DVD's.

Some of your shared scenes with Arthur English (Slugger) were quite comedic – what was he like to work with?
Arthur was terrific – a natural comic. Together we would devise a little piece of comedy to work into a scene, and it kind of balanced out the intense scenes between Dora and Steve.

***Jack Cardiff directing Arthur English (Slugger) in a scene from* The Hundred Pound Horse**

Series 2

Episode 1	Someone Somewhere
Episode 2	The Debt
Episode 3	Family of Strangers
Episode 4	Present for Sandy
Episode 5	The Innocents
Episode 6	The Hundred Pound Horse
Episode 7	Poor Bald Head
Episode 8	The Prize
Episode 9	Treasure Hunt
Episode 10	Debt of Honour
Episode 11	Out-of-the-Blue Horse
Episode 12	The Awakening
Episode 13	Fly Away Home

Episode 1: Someone, Somewhere

Directed by Claude Whatham

The Story

Steve is in Liverpool looking for his mother, who is in debt and wanted by the police. Dora is trying to trace the owner of a horse that the police have brought to Follyfoot Farm. Her search leads to the Leeds and Liverpool Canal, which reminds her of Steve whom she is missing.

Steve and Dora each believe that someone, somewhere has to care. Steve sets out to find his mother and Dora, the owner of the horse.

**Dora and Hercules
(Travelling Lady)**

The same location 40 years later

My Story

Well there we were again back at Follyfoot Farm. Copper and the other permanent horses were settled in their stables and the Horse Girls had settled into their new quarters. The horses had wintered well and were all passed fit by the vet.

The horse we used for this episode was Travelling Lady, who belonged to Cyril (Mr Townend) whose farm we had used in the first series in the *Gypsy* episode. One of the stories he told us about Lady was that when he rode to the pub she would wait outside for him. If he came out a little drunk, Lady always got him home no matter what. Somehow, Cyril would still manage to take the tack off and put her in a nice warm stable, and when asked about his night out the following morning, he would not remember much about it. Cyril was always a great teller of stories, but I like to believe this one was true.

April that year at Follyfoot Farm was wet, cold and miserable, but filming had to go on regardless.

Lady was very old and it showed on her face, which was going grey. She also had a docked tail, which was not allowed anymore by law. Filming was done near Dobson Lock, Apperley Bridge, on the Leeds Liverpool Canal, and Lady, called Hercules in the script, had to go up to a barge and stay there to receive titbits. To make her stay near the barge a Horse Girl was on the ground holding her so she would not run away until required. Lady did give us a bit of surprise when she was being chased by Dora. She really seemed to be enjoying herself and despite her age, covered a lot of the open fields along the canal. We had a long gap in between takes whilst we caught her and brought her back.

The lock keeper's cottage had a makeover specially for filming. Shutters and a trellis were put on, white stones placed round the flowerbeds at the front – all to make it look good on camera. The cottage used was actually not near the canal, but near Apperley Bridge.

Steve, supposedly in Liverpool, was actually filmed in Leeds in the back-to-back terraces that used to be numerous in the city. The 'Liverpool' section of the canal was actually filmed near Leeds city centre.

Bargee (Harry Littlewood)

Episode 2: The Debt

Directed by Claude Whatham

The Story

Steve is still in Liverpool working to pay off his mother's debt. Meanwhile, Dora is looking after a pony called Jonas, whose owner decides to put him back to work taking newsprint rolls to the Gazette. Jonas is not up to this and so the owner borrows Pride, a horse which belongs to a friend of the Colonel.

Steve earns enough money to pay off his mother's debt but is sadly let down when she spends the money on a night out with the girls. A disillusioned Steve returns to Follyfoot and an emotional Dora.

My Story

On the first day of filming there was heavy snow on the ground, but luckily when we came to shoot the scenes with the horses it had gone. This was the sort of day when the bacon butties from Kennedy's (the location caterers) went down a real treat.

Jonas returns to Follyfoot

Jonas and Pride, the horses chosen for this episode, were both good in harness and very reliable as the actor (Leslie Dwyer) had not done much work with horses. He had to learn quickly how to drive a horse and cart. The Horse Girls were always within grabbing distance of the reins in case either horse got frightened by the cameras or the lights. When Jonas had to stand particularly still in one scene a Horse Girl was standing out of shot at his head.

A scene was shot in Leeds Docks where Pride was frightened by its owner, backed up towards the river and the newsprint roll fell off into the water. To make this happen, a large log was placed at the edge of the wharf, the wheels of the cart hit it and the specially made lightweight roll fell off.

It was a wrap. The horses we used were taken back to their owners and we skipped out to feed and water the horses not used for filming. If we had not had time to exercise them earlier in the day we would then do so.

It was then time to go to the Studios to get showered, have something to eat and more importantly a drink in the YTV bar! Later I went to see the rushes of the day's shooting with Tony Essex, the episode director and the actors. Sometimes I could spot mistakes with the horses, such as a Horse Girl's hand being in shot. However, we had very clever editors who managed to put these right, most of the time!

The Colonel and Dora arrive at the docks

Episode 3: Family of Strangers

Directed by Desmond Davis

The Story

Dora's friend Cleo, who was the best rider at their school and competed at Showing and Jumping, arrives to stay at Follyfoot. She does not ride anymore and never will, because of an accident her sister had when a horse tried to trample her to death. Ron, Dora and Steve plan to help Cleo get her nerve back. The ploy becomes a reality when Steve gets his foot caught in a trap and Cleo has to ride Copper to get help.

My Story

Harvey Smith, the famous show jumper, wintered his horses in one of the fields next to Follyfoot Farm. One of his horses was a big grey gelding called Warpaint. The weather was still really wet and cold so I thought it would be nice to bring him into some warmth in our stables. I rang Harvey and told him what I had done, and he was not pleased. He said I was doing Warpaint more harm than good, as he was now retired and lived out in the field permanently. I then had the cheek to ask him if we could use him for filming. To my surprise he said 'yes' as long as we did not do any riding shots with him. I guess we did cheat a little because Cleo was led into the yard riding bare-back on Warpaint. Perhaps Harvey missed that episode!

Dora had to lunge Copper (exercise the horse in a circle on a lunge line) but when she had a lot of dialogue, Copper would be taken away and one of the Horse Girls would pretend to be the horse and pull on the line out of shot. This was done mainly for close-ups so that nothing got in the way of the camera or lights.

Me after ringing Harvey Smith

Steve placing his foot in the trap prior to filming

Episode 4: Present for Sandy

Directed by Desmond Davis

The Story

While exercising Alex, Steve comes across a cottage on fire. He helps the old lady by getting an ambulance but she later dies in hospital. He hears a horse whinnying near the burning cottage and goes to investigate. Steve takes the horse, Cavalier, back to Follyfoot Farm and is accused of stealing it. A father and his daughter-in-law each claim to be the owner. Dora and Steve eventually discover the father is secretly training the horse as a suitable ride and birthday gift for his grandson Sandy.

Dora had always dreamed of having a horse as a birthday gift and ensures that this becomes a reality for Sandy.

Steve to the rescue

My Story

The fire scene was filmed at a derelict farmer's cottage between Harewood and Harrogate. Once again the building was plastered with the special sticky brown paste to prevent damage to the existing building.

For the fire scene we hired a local ambulance and crew to use for filming and also had a fire engine standing by in case of any emergency.

Arden Tints, the horse we used to play Cavalier, was owned by my friend Jackie Stone (later she became one of the Horse Girls). We really had to be careful with Tints because she was a county show hack and worth lots of money. She was also a thoroughbred, which meant she could be quite spirited. Tints was not put in the shed until the fire scene had been shot and the fire at the cottage had been put out. The derelict shed was very dark and a bit spooky, but she eventually settled enough for action to be called and the cameras to roll.

The location for the birthday party was once again at Cyril Townend's in Shadwell. Tony Essex really liked filming there because of its great character and he also felt it portrayed a typical Yorkshire Farm.

Sandy's birthday party

Episode 5: The Innocents

Directed by Desmond Davis

The Story

The miners at the local colliery are out on strike. Dora hears from Tom Platt, who worked with One White-Foot Charley (Series One), that to publicise their cause, the miners have left three pit ponies underground that they are not feeding. Dora is told the situation is very delicate but still decides to help rescue the ponies even though the Colonel tells her not to get involved. With the help of some sympathetic miners the ponies are rescued.

Me collecting ponies from the pit

On the tunnel set constructed at the pit-head

My Story

Tony Essex asked me to go to the studios to discuss an idea he had for one of the episodes. He had heard that some pit ponies were being brought up for the last time from a nearby pit at Castleford and were to be retired to good homes. Tony had arranged for me to go and see them with a view to buying them for filming. I visited the mine where the ponies were in the stables above ground. The stables were spotless and the ponies in really good condition and well fed on lots of oats. When I led them out they were really frisky. I must say, the miners loved their ponies and they became very close working in the pits together. The Coal Board insisted that the RSPCA approve the conditions at Follyfoot Farm before we were given permission to buy them, and also insisted that they were never to be ridden. We passed the RSPCA test and the ponies came to be stars in the series.

Farmer, Boxer and Paddy all had individual characters. A good example of this was Boxer. Whilst we mucked out the stables, the ponies were allowed to roam in the yard. The muck heap was built in three step-like layers that went up to the height of the yard wall. One morning Boxer decided he was bored and climbed up the muck heap steps, jumped over the wall into the field and then decided he was going to play with Harvey Smith's horses, chasing them as if to say 'look at me – I'm so clever'.

To do the night shoot at the pit, we took all three ponies. A miner came up to the horsebox to look at them and told us he had worked in the pit with a pony. Suddenly, to our amazement we heard a yell, 'It's him, it's him, it's Farmer, it's my old pony!' It was so moving I cried; he was so happy to see his old working companion and so pleased to know

The ponies are returned to the mine

he had a good home and was also going to be famous.

For safety reasons we were not allowed to take the film lights down into the pit as any electrical equipment had to be specially sealed to prevent the risk of sparking. Desmond Davis, the Director, decided to build a set of the mine tunnel at the pit head cages. We were allowed to film a little way underground in the lift cage with the ponies and actors, who had to wear special safety gear and were checked for cigarettes and lighters. The Horse Girls were worried that the retired ponies might be distressed by being put back in the pit lift cage. Not at all, they were not in the least bit fazed. Just as well perhaps, for there was no room in the cage for a Horse Girl!

Episode 6: The Hundred Pound Horse

Directed by Jack Cardiff

The Story

Tim Shaw (Marc Granger) has a pony called Periwinkle and lives with his father on the travelling Fairground, which is currently near Follyfoot. Tim takes Periwinkle to see Dora as his father Geoff (Keith Buckley) has threatened to have him shot because he costs too much to feed and does not earn his keep. Tim tells Dora that Periwinkle once won the Grand National and is therefore very special. Dora helps Tim to get the pony fit for racing but Ron tells him the pony is useless. Tim runs away with the pony, but eventually comes back to Follyfoot Farm where Steve persuades Tim to return home to the Fair.

Tim on Periwinkle

My Story

Periwinkle was a pony with feathers (long hair at the bottom of its fetlocks) and therefore not at all like a Grand National horse but, like Tim, we all have dreams. Periwinkle turned out to be a very safe, but quite lazy horse and the young actor playing Tim had to work hard, with our help, to get him galloping.

The travelling fair used in filming this episode was specially created, and was filmed in open space on Scott Hall Road. We Horse Girls were used as some of the extras to go on the rides. This was really good fun and a bit of relaxation for us as there were very few horses to look after in this episode.

Tim and Dora

Geoff Shaw, Steve and Slugger at the Fairground

Episode 7: Poor Bald Head

Directed by Michael Apted

The Story

The Colonel decides there are too many horses at Follyfoot and tells Dora to sell Tammany. Dora loves all of them and does not want to let any of them go. Steve and Dora plot to make Tammany rather wild and therefore not suitable for sale to the solicitor's (David Swift) daughter Wendy (Elaine Donnelly). The local coalman (John Barrett) is working his Shire horse, Ranger, too hard. Dora wants to rescue it but there is no room at Follyfoot unless Tammany is sold to Wendy. To lead into the following episode the story has Steve developing a friendship with Wendy, which rather upsets Dora.

The coalman and Ranger

I did not know anyone with a Shire horse and cart so the props buyer found one (at least the Unions were pleased!). The people who owned him stayed right next to him for all the film action, even sometimes being seen in shot riding on the cart.

Tammany was played by Steve's usual ride, Alex. We quite regularly used some of our horses as different characters in different episodes. Alex also appeared as a double for Moonstone (Series 1, Episode 8).

To make Alex play up in the stable, the Horse Girls were on the floor rustling the lunge whip in the straw to make him kick out. Poor Steve had to pull him round in circles out in the yard and try to make him look wild, but Alex was not feeling wild that day. Maybe it was too warm.

The final sequence was only effective on screen due to Steve's efforts, clever camera angles and sharp editing. In the final scene Alex was supposed to be well-behaved but he was 'napping' (misbehaving) and moving towards the gate for home, where he clearly wanted to be. Hopefully no viewers noticed.

It's nice to know that our horses were generally so contented. The Horse Girls and cast all had to work very hard to make them appear discontented when the plot required!

My favourite picture of Steve on Alex

Episode 8: The Prize

Directed by Jack Cardiff

The Story

Steve is giving riding lessons to Wendy who is now the owner of Tammany. Dora is not happy about this but is busy organising a show to be held at the Colonel's house (actually Stockeld Park near Spofforth). Steve asks if Wendy can take part in the Cross Country Event and Dora reluctantly agrees. Tammany does not complete the Cross Country so Steve asks Wendy to tea and then gives her a riding lesson. Dora is upset about Steve and Wendy, and about one of her ponies, Kalinka, who is going blind. Wendy lets slip how Steve feels about Dora and she also gives Dora a gift as there is no prize for the winner of the Cross Country, which Dora wins.

Mummy carrying on as though nothing is wrong

Gymkhana day

My Story

We were lucky it was a fine and sunny day for filming the Gymkhana scenes at Stockeld Park. We had a lot of ponies and young riders as well as the older riders and horses for the Cross Country. I had asked a lot of friends with children who had ponies if they would like to take part. By now Follyfoot was a very well known and popular TV series, so not surprisingly, they all wanted to be involved.

This was one of the few episodes when we used more than one camera because of all the action. It would have been very difficult to repeat the scenes and very time consuming. In the Gymkhana scene, one mother was helping her little boy, who was still on a leading rein, to mount his pony. She did not realise that she was treading on his foot at the same time and he began to cry. She quickly got off his foot and put him, still crying, onto the pony as if nothing had happened. I must admit, in the evening, watching the rushes, this caused lots of laughter and it was decided to leave it in.

In the Cross Country Race it was decided to use Sirocco, who was very fast, as a double for Copper in the distance shots. The horses looked very similar except for Copper's distinctive four white legs and white mark on his stomach. We wrapped red protective bandages on Sirocco's legs to hide where the white marking was. This worked well until there was a close-up shot of Dora actually riding Copper and guess what – no red bandages but four white legs! Another deliberate mistake!

Episode 9: Treasure Hunt

Directed by Gerry Mill

The Story

Two sisters, Agnes and Emily Derwent (Dorothea Rundle and Betty Turner), who live in a big house, no longer get on. One of them is ill and cannot look after her horse, Delilah. Dora is asked by the Colonel to bring it to Follyfoot Farm. Delilah will not eat and Dora is also not eating because she is pining over Steve's friendship with Wendy. Steve suggests Delilah is taken back to her home and Dora and he will take turns to look after her. As they ride to Follyfoot Farm, Steve tells Dora about his Grandma and her belief that life is like a treasure hunt. We all go through our lives collecting treasures, such as special moments, and people or places, to remember when we are old. This is how he would like it to be between Dora and himself, just to keep on as they are, because really their lives are worlds apart.

The sick sister goes into hospital and after talking with Steve and Dora the sisters end their feud.

The warring Derwent sisters – Agnes with Dora

My Story

I have already mentioned the Edwards girls and this episode was mainly shot at their house in Pately Bridge. It was very big and was run as a trekking centre. The set designers moved in with the props buyers and divided the house interior into two sets.

It was Autumn and across from the property were beautiful woods. The Director liked the view so much he created a scene at the beginning of the episode with Dora exercising Copper, trotting and cantering through the leaves. When Dora was trying to get Delilah to eat we did not use bran but wet sawdust. Before the shot, a Horse Girl would tempt her with a handful, so that on the actual take, Delilah knew it was not edible and would therefore turn her nose up at it. On many occasions throughout the series, Gillian and Steve would fasten their horses by their reins to railings, gates or anything they could find. Let me assure you, a Horse Girl was always on hand just out of shot to take hold of the horse, in case of a problem. We nearly had one nasty accident in this situation, but I will tell you about that in the episode in which it happened, later on in the book.

Emily with Steve and Dora

Episode 10: Debt of Honour

Directed by Eric Price

The Story

Steve and Dora are out riding when a man waving some papers frightens Copper, who gallops off and treads on some glass, cutting his foot. They walk to Carne Manor, the home of Lady Carne, an old friend of the Colonel. They leave Copper at the stables until they can collect him with the horsebox. The man who caused the accident is a bookmaker chasing Ron for a debt. Ron has given him a false address, but when out riding on his bike he is stopped by the debt collector and told he has until the next day to pay.

Lady Carne (Ambrosine Phillpotts) rides over to Follyfoot on Jellico, her only asset, and asks Dora to look after him and let no one know he is there. If anyone asks, Dora is to change his name as Lady Carne is also in debt to the same bookmaker.

Ron tries to steal Jellico to pay off his debt and hides him in the old shed by the lake. He pretends to cripple the horse to make him worthless, tricking the bookie into returning his IOU. Lady Carne settles her gambling debt of honour by selling her house but keeping Jellico, and the Colonel makes Ron pay up as well.

The Colonel gets Ron to pay up

My Story

This episode was filmed at a large estate near Wetherby. We used the grounds, the stables and the house. In the opening shot Steve and Dora are cantering in the grounds. When they had to canter across the drive, Copper, with Horse Girl Gillian riding as Dora's double, actually slipped and came down on his knees, grazing them and causing a bit of swelling. I remember Tony Essex wanted to include it in the episode but I said no as it was quite a bad accident and Copper could not gallop for later scenes. This prompted us to get a 'look-alike' so we went back to Mount Pleasant Stud and acquired Saber. He turned out to be a bit of a disaster all round but that is another story. Often the scenes were shot out of sequence so fortunately we had already filmed the scene of Copper with his cut foot.

Lady Carne's horse, Jellico, belonged to one of my friends and was a retired hunter. In his younger days he had been a show hunter. For one of the scenes I was asked to make him appear really lame, but of course without hurting him. The only thing I could think of was to 'rug him up' using a surcingle. This is a device used to fasten a rug over a horse. I then tied a piece of cotton to his foot and attached another piece of plaiting cotton from the foot to the surcingle. This allowed Jellico to put his toe to the ground but not his whole foot. The horse was amazing; at first I made the plaiting cotton too short but he did not get worried or frightened, and I was standing by with a pair of sharp scissors to cut the cotton if he did. Sadly, in some of the shots you could see the cotton but I probably noticed it more because I knew it was there.

After the scene Jellico walked off as right as rain, just as Dora said.

Ron leading the lame Jellico from the shed

Episode 11: Out-of-the-Blue Horse

Directed by Peter Hammond

The Story

Callie (previously seen in Series 1, Episode 8, Moonstone) is being threatened with boarding school. She wants Dora to let Magic, her pony, stay at Follyfoot, or she will fail her entrance exam on purpose. Dora has to tell her that the Colonel says Follyfoot is full.

Callie knows of a stable where she may be able to take Magic, but when she and Dora get there they are upset to discover Ladybird, in very bad condition.

Dora involves the Colonel and Steve, who nearly comes to blows with the owner of the pony whose disabled wife teaches at Callie's school. Her husband is trying to use the ill pony as a means of getting their estranged daughter home.

Callie deliberately fails the exam in order to keep Magic. She then writes an essay in which she tells the story of Steve and Ladybird. The teacher reads it and persuades her husband to send Ladybird to Follyfoot, where the Colonel has decided to build more stalls to accommodate more horses.

Ladybird in her shed

Ladybird in full make-up

My Story

For this episode we needed an old pony that could be made up to look neglected and in really bad condition. Once again, a friend, Pat Rushworth, came to the rescue with her old pony Tiffany.

Pat Swords, our make-up artist, put gel on Tiffany (Ladybird) to make the coat look matted, and added patches of fake blood to show where sores had appeared. I mixed some Fullers Earth into a paste and painted it along where the pony's ribs were. This made Tiffany (Ladybird) look very thin, as though the ribs were showing.

Some months later, I found the pony that played Ladybird lying in her stable and she did not seem able to stand. I called the owner, who told me to ring her vet. He came and took some blood tests and said he thought the pony was very ill. After we had nursed the pony all night he rang to tell us he thought the pony had a disease which was not supposed to be in the UK, and that we would have to inform the Ministry of Agriculture. They would probably require us to stop filming straightaway. He also suggested that all our horses were at risk and could die.

I rang Tony Essex who not surprisingly nearly blew a fuse and told me to get our own vet out straight away for a second opinion. Luckily he was much more reassuring – and correct, as it turned out to be a false alarm. Tony still wanted the pony out of Follyfoot immediately. I recently found out from Pat Rushworth that Tiffany had been suffering from a blood disorder (anaemia).

Episode 12: The Awakening

Directed by Desmond Davis

The Story

Lord Beck (Anthony Andrews) comes to stay with the Colonel. Dora and Steve are invited for tea but Ron thinks the Colonel is match making, which does not please her. Dora changes in to her oldest jeans to make a bad impression in front of Lord Beck. Dora is concerned about the health of the Colonel and avoids the tea party, where Steve makes a bet that Copper can beat Lord Beck's horse, Champion of Beck. The Colonel persuades Dora to accept the challenge in the hope of teaching the arrogant Lord Beck a lesson and bringing him down a peg or two.

On the day of the show Copper and Champion of Beck are neck and neck when the Colonel is taken ill. Dora pulls up Copper to find out what is happening and loses the competition. Lord Beck is gracious enough to say Copper would have won because he can see she trains her horses with kindness.

Anthony Andrews as Lord Beck

My Story

I enjoyed making this episode more than any other. The episode was filmed in the fields near Follyfoot and the show jumping course was designed and built by Andrew Fielder, another friend and a well-known international show jumper. He had also helped me with the training of Copper and my own horse. The Director told me he would work with Andrew and I at any time with horses. It was a great compliment to us both, but really we were only doing for Follyfoot what we enjoyed doing best in real life.

Gillian Croft, one of the Horse Girls, rode Copper as Dora's double and, believe it or not, I doubled for Lord Beck! Gillian had to wear a latex mask modelled from Dora's face. This meant her going to London for the fitting. I admired her for riding in the uncomfortable mask, because I would have found it claustrophobic and could not have handled it. All I had to do was have a moustache put on and have the upper part of my body tightly bandaged so that I did not look too much like a girl on film.

Anthony Andrews was a very good rider and could easily have done the scene himself. However, the filming insurance conditions ruled that out. Champion of Beck was actually Sky, my own horse. It had been suggested that a stunt rider be employed but because Anthony knew how much I loved my horse he suggested that I be allowed to be his double. I remember when a fence had to be knocked down, all I had to do was tweak down the right rein at the appropriate time and Sky would knock the pole off on cue. The Director was really pleased because this meant we got it in one take.

At the beginning of *Follyfoot* my horse had been lamed with a very badly-pulled tendon. It was extra special for me to have her fit and able to jump again. It had taken nearly a year to get her well, with regular trips to the seaside to walk, and eventually canter Sky in the seawater. I am positive this really helped her recovery.

Me as Lord Beck

Attaching my moustache

Follyfoot Remembered: Anthony Andrews (Lord Beck)

Anthony Andrews as Lord Beck

Apologies for not writing sooner but I was abroad, and my letter writing suffered.

My only memory is that, although Jane Royston did a fabulous job in doubling for me, I was sorry not to be able to do my own jumping, as I had show-jumped from an early age – it is often the case that actors can't get insured to take risks regardless of their skills!

I do recall all the cast who were so good, and particularly Christian who I had known before. Please pass on my very good wishes.

Yours

Episode 13: Fly Away Home

Directed by Desmond Davis

The Story

The Colonel is very ill and Dora's parents (played by Basil Henson and Dorothy Reynolds) are recalled from abroad. Dora is worried that her stay at Follyfoot Farm may be coming to an end and she may have to leave with her parents. She takes them to Follyfoot Farm, which her mother hates. Her father meets Ladybird who won't go to the field but prefers to stay in her stable where she feels wanted and loved. Equally Dora does not want to leave Follyfoot where she feels really at home and where she also is wanted and loved. Steve tells her father how Ladybird's story is also the story of Dora.

Thanks to this conversation, her father agrees that Dora can stay and hopes he can come to see her more often and get to know her better. The Colonel decides to give Follyfoot Farm to Dora making her Mistress of Follyfoot. Leaves sprouting on the Lightning Tree are seen as a good omen.

Dora's parents visit Follyfoot

My Story

Two of the ponies used in this episode were former pit ponies, Farmer and Boxer. The location of the flower shop was in the village of Thorner. When he was outside the flower shop, Farmer took a huge liking to eating the flowers. Luckily they did not do him any harm. At one stage Christian had to let go of Farmer, who then disappeared out of shot, though Boxer hid the disappearance quite well. Farmer had decided to go off on a stroll down a nearby drive; luckily, a Horse Girl was on hand.

Arthur English (Slugger), Desmond Llewelyn (Colonel) and Gillian Blake (Dora) in a scene from Fly Away Home

Steve, Dora's father, Dora and Ladybird

The Lightning Tree had earlier grown leaves and we had to call in the local fire brigade to remove them. Sadly, when we needed leaves on the tree it did not oblige and we had to stick some on!

During the filming I often felt as though I was watching some of my own life story, but slightly changed. Tony Essex and I had often talked about my life and my feelings; about how I was the black sheep of our family; and how my love of horses (which I am sorry to have to admit) came above everybody and everything else. Not forgetting my love for my 'secret' farm which had become Follyfoot.

In Conversation with Steve Hodson (Steve)

Steve Hodson

When you auditioned for the role of Steve, did you meet any of the other cast?

I did a film test at Hollin Hall with Gillian and Christian. We were filmed riding horses and generally interacting with each other. I originally didn't get the part – it went to actor Robin Stewart whose character's name was Paul. I think Robin was working on the first two episodes when it was decided to replace him, and I was told I had got the part. The character's name was changed to Steve and the two episodes were re-shot. I was living in London at the time so I moved back to Bradford where my parents lived. When I was filming, my father use to drop me off at the Yorkshire Television studios. From there, a coach would take most of the cast and crew down to the Follyfoot location. As the series progressed I did buy my own car – an Austin Cambridge which I nicknamed Geoffrey! I don't know much about cars, but I do enjoy the freedom and independence that

Steve Hodson

Steve Hodson with Alex

they give you. Having my own car meant being able to go off somewhere just when I felt like it. Horses are part of that feeling – that's why I liked to ride as often as I could, apart from just for the series.

Did you have an outline of the character?
The casting director provided me with an outline of Steve's character, but a lot of it was detailed in the book *Cobbler's Dream*.

As the series progressed, did you become aware how popular the show was becoming?
Probably not straight away because we had filmed several of the episodes before they were transmitted, so there would have been a delay before getting the viewers' reactions. I think initially I was given a three-month contract, with an option to extend. I do remember winning a best actor award from Germany for Follyfoot, and they arranged a presentation for me in the UK – VIP's were invited, and I forgot to go – completely forgot!

Steve Hodson with 'Geoffrey'

When you were nearing the end of the third series was there any mention of a fourth?
No, Tony Essex was involved in his next project Luke's Kingdom, *and Gillian and I were to take the lead roles. For various reasons it didn't happen and my role was taken by Oliver Tobias. There was going to be a* Follyfoot *feature film, and I did see the first draft of the proposed film script. I know it was going to be directed by David Hemmings, but I can't recall the story line. It was never made, partly I think because of lack of suitable finances.*

Follyfoot *was sold to over twenty countries – what response was there from fans?*
There was an amazing response from the UK, and I know the series

was very popular in Europe, Australia and New Zealand. In the beginning Yorkshire Television had been managing my fan mail, but it became too much for them so they asked me if I could take it on. I couldn't cope with it and I was approached by a lady called Eileen from a magazine that ran my fan club. I think she charged about 50p a time to join, and she issued newsletters and kept the fans up to date with what I was doing. I think she is probably a multi-millionaire by now!!

Tony Essex was executive producer and scriptwriter – how would you describe him?
Definitely a workaholic and the real driving force behind the series – he would usually appear on set if there was a problem.

While filming Follyfoot you recorded a single called Crystal Bay – how did that come about?
Yorkshire Television had a subsidiary recording label called York Records which was part of the Decca group. Follyfoot had quite a high profile, and I was approached about the possibility of recording a song called Crystal Bay, which was written by Maurice Gibb and Billy Lawrie (Lulu's brother). To be honest I wasn't that keen on the song, but there was mention of a follow-up album and I was really keen to do some blues numbers. I was flown

Steve Hodson as Steve Ross

Valerie Holliman (Cleo) in a scene from **Family of Strangers**

down to London from Leeds and spent a couple of days in the recording studio, which I really enjoyed. I also met Lulu, who was there recording backing tracks for the single.

Does any particular episode or scene from the series remain in your memory?

I remember an episode from the second series called The Innocents *directed by Desmond Davis. The story line concerned the plight of some pit ponies that Dora thought had been abandoned and left down the mine. We were filming on location at Thornhill Colliery and in the lunch break I went down the actual mine to the coal face. It was a real eye opener, so dark and cold, and I was trying to imagine what it would have been like to work down there. Another episode I remember was called* Family of Strangers, *again from the second series. Actress Valerie Holliman was playing the part of Cleo. We had been at drama school together, although I think she was a year or two behind me. Anyway, she was on set and she fainted so I had to carry her back to the dressing room.*

You rode a horse called *Alex* in several of the episodes – what happened to him after the series ended?

Alex was an Appaloosa, a breed descended from war-mounts used by the Plain Indians of North America and, like a lot of the horses when the series ended, he was sold to a private buyer. I do know that his new owner rode Alex from John O'Groats to Lands End in aid of charity. Alex played several different roles in various episodes, and because he was so well behaved he was kept for the series. He was almost fifteen hands

***Steve Hodson (Steve) and Alastair Hunter (Carlton) filming a scene from* The Distant Voice**

Gillian Blake and Steve Hodson

83

high, and provided an ideal contrast with Gillian's horse Copper, *who was a really striking chestnut Arab cross.*

Does any Follyfoot fan mail still filter through to you?
Yes it does. I get letters and, more recently, e-mails – which I do read!

Did you ever revisit the farm after the series ended?
Yes, I went back a couple of years later and did a photo shoot for a magazine.

How did you enjoy working with Gillian?
I really enjoyed working with Gillian. We got on really well, and worked together again after the series ended, appearing in a couple of stage plays.

You have worked on television and radio – what is your preferred medium?
I love radio – just me and a microphone. These days I work on Talking Books for the blind and radio plays, as well as teaching drama students. When I am not working I like to read, visit art galleries and write poetry.

Steve Hodson (Steve) *in a scene from* **Rain on Friday**

Series 3

Episode 1	The Distant Voice
Episode 2	The Four-Legged Hat
Episode 3	Barney
Episode 4	Miss Him When He's Gone
Episode 5	The Dream
Episode 6	The Challenge
Episode 7	The Letter
Episode 8	The Bridge Builder
Episode 9	Uncle Joe
Episode 10	The Helping Hand
Episode 11	Rain on Friday
Episode 12	Hazel
Episode 13	Walk in the Wood

Episode 1: The Distant Voice

Directed by Stephen Frears

The Story

Dora is now the owner of Follyfoot Farm and overrides Steve to bring in Tansy, a pony belonging to a friend of the Colonel. But there is a problem – the pony has strangles, which is very infectious and also a killer. Dora has twin ponies to school but when the owner finds out about the strangles, he takes them away.

The Colonel agrees with what Dora has done and arranges for two more horses to come in for schooling from Major Lewis's yard. Steve and Dora make up when she explains to him she did not make the decision to bring in Tansy just to make the point that she was boss. She simply wanted to help, and to give Tansy a chance of life.

Dora in the donkey pen nursing Tansy

Steve and the twins (count the legs!)

My Story

It was now the third year of filming at Follyfoot Farm and our winter break at the Harrison's Stables had come to an end. The Horse Girls and myself were ready for action, or at least we thought so. It seemed strange that some of the filming was done at Harrison's, Tansy's original home.

The Donkey Pen had a face lift by the set designers and poor Bubble and Squeak, the donkeys, had to go out in the field, which they thoroughly enjoyed. We did not enjoy it because they were very nervous and hard to catch.

Sadly, I cannot remember where the twin ponies came from, but I have a feeling our prop buyer found them. All I do remember is the owner was very watchful over what we did, because it is quite rare to have twins that survive after birth.

I would just like to say that these days, if a horse gets strangles the vet will advise that no horse or pony should go off the yard, or come onto the yard. In addition, all owners and staff should not go to shows or anywhere to do with horses, until the yard has been given the all clear by the vet after blood tests are clear. It is also known that some horses can be carriers and not show any symptoms, so very often they are blood tested as well.

Episode 2: The Four-Legged Hat

Directed by Gareth Davies

The Story

Dora has just bought a new day rug for Copper but sadly she has no money to pay for it. She says she will pay next month, but on the way home she passes a shop with a lovely blue hat in the window and looks at it longingly. Suddenly, she sees an old pony, Domino, pulling a cart which is laden with wood and much too heavy. Dora offers the owner, Clem Barrett, the loan of Hercules in exchange for Domino until he finds another horse. Clem insists he wants ten pounds. Dora agrees and has to borrow the money from Slugger, so now she owes ten pounds. However, the price goes up again and again until it gets to thirty pounds. Clem takes Hercules to the horse sales where he tries to sell him but is caught in the act by Dora and Ron. They eventually get the Colonel, who was there on behalf of the RSPCA, to buy Domino whom they had exchanged with Hercules. She has the hat on loan but decides to send it back.

Gillian and the infamous hat

My Story

Gareth Davies, the Director, said he wanted an authentic old pony to play the part of Domino. He had heard that there was some horse sales in Lancashire and said he would like to go so he could choose the pony. This was fine by me because it meant a day out and I knew I could leave the day's filming in the Horse Girls' capable hands.

We arrived at the sales on a dull day and it was really quite miserable. Gareth spotted exactly what he wanted. The pony was in an outside pen and its nose was nearly touching the ground. With its harness on it looked so sad, and I told Gareth we could not buy the pony, because it would be cruel. It did not look as if it would last the day. I lost the discussion and we bought Domino for twelve pounds and the harness for thirty. That tells you everything – the harness having cost more than the pony. I still was not happy about the situation but Gareth said that was what the *Follyfoot* series was all about. I had to agree, but I would rather have kept it in the scripts and not for real.

It was then time to go home. I took the pony's harness to lead it out of the pen and it set off with me. Suddenly, I had this little tank engine. I pulled him up and just had to laugh. This pony was the best actor of the lot and no longer did I feel we were being cruel. The previous owner told us his real name was Black Beauty and would we drive up to his house with the Land Rover and trailer so his children could say goodbye? They were all thrilled that their old pony was going to be a film star. When we put him in the trailer he would only travel with his head hanging over the back ramp so he could see what was happening. He really was a great character.

The auction market we used for filming was at Pannal and belonged to the Robinson's from Bedale. We filmed on a Saturday when the real auction was on, and on another day when nothing was happening. On that occasion the pens were disinfected with Jeyes Fluid and bedded down with straw. The ponies from Follyfoot were staying the night so we could commence filming the next day at the crack of dawn. It seemed quite sad seeing our ponies in the sales pens but we did make them as comfortable as possible.

Slugger also tries a new hat!

Follyfoot Remembered: John Cater (Clem Barratt)

I haven't thought of *Follyfoot* for about thirty years and it's good to be reminded of that extraordinary job. Extraordinary mainly because of the exec. producer, Tony Essex. He was a well-known maker of documentary film, his best known being *The Great War* series with Laurence Olivier speaking the commentary. Clips from this are still widely used in TV history programmes.

Essex was brilliant and an eccentric, but he knew nothing about actors or acting. Unfortunately, he frequently appeared on the location sets making silly suggestions – sometimes still in his carpet slippers! The post-synchronisation sound system was bizarre and never used before or since: with no guiding picture-track, one listened to one's original sound track on headphones and had to dub the new speech exactly in tandem with the old; very difficult and impractical, as lip-synch is the tried and tested method used over decades. In spite of the digital sound recording system in current use it is still the norm.

I think I got the job, as always, via my agent but mainly because I was an old mate of the director, Gareth Davies. I had acted with him in Ipswich Rep in the fifties. And I worked with him years later in *Darling Buds of May*. Jobs literally

John Cater (Clem Barrett) in The Four Legged Hat

dropped through the letter-box in those days. Not so now! Even established names have to slog up to some dingy office in Soho to be grilled by a posse of producers, writers and casting directors. I have to go through the same humiliating process for a two-page part in some load of rubbish and sometimes, frankly, I can't be bothered to turn up.

I was genuinely thrilled to be with Arthur English whom I'd admired since his *Variety Bandbox* days on radio; his fast-talking Cockney spiv act was a joy. Arthur was a nice man and loved talking, which suited me.

Peter Whitbread, who played the auctioneer, was a chum from RADA days and another eccentric. On tour, he lived in an old post-office van which contained his kitchen, his bedroom, his books and his upright piano. It may have been during *Follyfoot* that a police car, hearing strange noises coming from a slightly rocking red van, stopped and one of the coppers knocked on the rear shutter. It was raised by a man in a velvet smoking-jacket, glass in hand and cigarette holder in mouth. Lit candles were fluttering in their holders on the front of the Victorian piano where a Mozart sonata, open on the music-rest, had been half played. Peter invited the police in for a nightcap and they readily accepted.

I am sure that story is exaggerated but I hope it's true in essence.

I remember nothing of my performance in *Four Legged Hat* – and indeed believe I've never heard of that title – except that when driving my cart through the village, it was filmed in Thorner, I used an old Cockney street cry. This should have been of northern vintage, but no one spotted the difference!

Peter Whitbread (Auctioneer) in **The Four Legged Hat**

Episode 3: Barney

Directed by Anthony R Thomas

The Story

The Buckleys are first-time horse buyers and come to Follyfoot Farm with a hope of finding one for their young daughter, Angela. Dora has nothing to sell so she goes with them to see a pony at Lockwood's, the horse dealer. There they are shown a horse called Dark Song, which Dora immediately says is not right.

A grey pony called Barney is brought out but seems too subdued, and again Dora and Steve suggest the Buckleys do not buy the pony, but sadly they do not take any notice and buy Barney.

Barney turns out to be a disaster, and so Dora brings him back to Follyfoot to be schooled and in the process falls in love with him. In the meantime the Buckleys buy Dark Song, but that does not work either and they decide to send him back to Lockwood's and take Barney home. Dora does not want this to happen, so Steve says that Barney will only behave when he is with Dora. Barney remains at Follyfoot and they also get Dark Song to school on condition he goes back when his schooling is completed.

Dolly running with stuntwoman Sadie Eddon

My Story

In this episode, Barney was originally bought from Pannal Auctions, and then we had the double which was a stunt horse called Dolly. This was organised by Reg Dent, who did the *Black Beauty* series and was very helpful when I had difficult scenes to do with the horses. As you know, our horses were just ordinary ponies and had never done anything like this before – like me really.

It was decided to do the filming of the Buckley's home on Black Moor Lane, Bardsey. Again the designers and the prop buyer went into action. A white fence was put up and a pre-fab hut in the field behind my friend's bungalow with, of course, permission from the local farmer. Gillian did a lot of her own stunt work but again, for close-up shots, somebody was pulling on the rope. However, she did do some of the rearing scenes, but for the dragging scene Sadie Eddon, the stunt rider, was called in.

Filming had finished at that location and we thought we had got all the shots we needed so the props, fencing, etc were taken down. However, Tony Essex then decided he wanted some more shots of the dragging scene. Unfortunately we could not get the original location due to the fact we had already ruined some of the farmer's hay and he was now in the process of cutting it. It was suggested we use our schooling paddock and put the prefab hut in the corner and nobody would be any wiser – except in the film, one minute the grass was really long and the next quite short. When Dora is schooling Barney and mounts for the first time, there is a rearing scene and as far as I can remember, Gillian did her own stunt riding on Dolly.

Dolly with stunt guy

The Buckleys buying Barney from Lockwood

Episode 4: Miss Him When He's Gone

Directed by Peter Hammond

The Story

Bobby belongs to an old man, Ed Foley, who is taken ill when on his rounds selling vegetables. His elder son, Brian, says he will take over the round but the old man says he will see Bobby dead first. The younger son takes Bobby to Follyfoot Farm for a few days and pretends to his family that he has run away. Meanwhile, at Follyfoot, Bobby is not eating and Dora is trying not to get too involved so she will not mind him going back. The police eventually come and Ron pretends he has just found Bobby wandering about in the fields. Dora takes Bobby back to his home where Ed, the old man, lets him out, sets the stable on fire and dies in the process.

Dora goes to collect Bobby and take him back to Follyfoot Farm.

Bobby and Ed Foley (John Barrie) making their deliveries

My Story

Bobby again came from Pannal Auction. He was a really good little pony. When we did the fire scene, fairly near the Yorkshire Television Studios he did not get scared. The fire was for real but we did have the fire brigade standing by to put it out as soon as we had finished filming. The stable was built by the set designers. It really was a spectacular fire and, as it was a cold night, was probably the only time we felt warm.

Richard Beaumont (Gavin Foley)

Ed Foley burns down the stable

Follyfoot Remembered: Richard Beaumont (Gavin Foley)

After watching the DVD it certainly stirred some memories!

I had a great time on *Follyfoot*. Firstly, Steve (Hodson) and I developed a mischievous streak in each other, and would regularly have 'food fights' between our scenes. This would involve us creeping up on each other, and thrusting a cream cake, or whatever, into each others faces. They were such a good bunch of actors who were passionate about the series – it was a privilege to work with them.

Gillian was wonderful to work with because, as a child actor, you can sometimes feel out of your depth, but Gillian always included me in the 'between takes' moments.

One of the biggest memories for me was the funeral scene, where we turned up on location to find that I didn't have a costume. We had to 'hire' trousers, shoes, shirt and coat from the crowd that had gathered to watch the filming, and I distinctly remember one mother asking for a fiver for me to wear her sons trousers!

The crew and cast were absolutely dedicated to their tasks in making *Follyfoot* a classic series, and I feel privileged to be a part (albeit small) of *Follyfoot*'s legacy.

Gillian Blake (Dora) and Richard Beaumont (Gavin) take a break from filming Miss Him When He's Gone

Richard Beaumont (Gavin) and Gillian Blake (Dora) filming the funeral scene from Miss Him When He's Gone

Episode 5: The Dream

Directed by Ken Hannam

The Story

The story is about a dispute between Clegg & Son and Lockwood's Riding School over land. Some motorbike riders chase Lockwood's horses, and one is killed and the others injured. Dora is having dreams which correspond with what is happening and Lockwood is blaming Clegg. The police want proof, so Lockwood puts the horses back hoping that it will happen again. Chip Lockwood comes to Follyfoot Farm to enquire who the girl is who has put in a complaint about his father and testifying on behalf of Clegg & Son. Of course it is Dora and he pleads for her not to do it. It turns out that Ron knows who the motorbike riders are but does not want to disclose the fact. Clegg's son threatens Dora not to give evidence in court and suggests that something will happen to her horses if she does. Ron, Steve and Dora go over to Clegg's and Steve has a fight with the son and tells Mr Clegg that the Colonel has fixed it that if he drops the case, Lockwood will sell him the land, all thanks to Chip.

Steve Hodson (Steve) and Colin Bell (Johnnie Clegg) in a scene from The Dream

My Story

I was dreading this episode because of the scene with the dead horse. I was told by Tony Essex that I had to get rid of all the Horse Girls. He did not want them to know at that time about using a horse that had just been put down and brought over for filming. It was to be draped over the fence by the second lake. I had asked the help of Peter Robinson from Pannal Auctions because I was not sure if I would be much good. Peter agreed as long as we could watch the Grand National if we had finished filming. The dead horse was draped over the barbed wire fence and then we took the other horses down. To my surprise they did not bother about the dead horse. We took part of the fence down to get them into the woods by the lake, and then replaced it and hoped some would jump it, which they did. We then put some food down to make the horses graze near to the dead horse.

One incident I recall was when I was asked to go and get something from the yard. I climbed into Cracker, the green Land Rover, got what I wanted and then, for some reason, decided to reverse. I heard a loud bang and wondered what on earth it was. I had only reversed into the one vehicle in the field and smashed the front! Little Cracker did not have a mark on her. Peter was really good and said he did not think I had caused too much damage. He took me out to dinner and did his best to cheer me up.

Monday morning arrived and I dared not get up to face Len Randall, who was a grip and the owner of the vehicle. He came into the caravan and, though he was upset, arranged for YTV to pay for the repairs. Tony Essex was only concerned that Little Cracker had not been damaged because it was used for filming. I told him it had only happened because of seeing the dead horse.

Gillian Blake (Dora) waiting to film a scene from The Dream

Episode 6: The Challenge

Directed by Jack Cardiff

The Story

Dora decides to have a day off and takes off on Copper. She meets Chip who tells her that his dad has organised a cross country race. The winner will receive £100, but Mr Lockwood has plans of winning himself with Chip riding one of his horses, Brigadier. Chip tells Dora that Copper might be a contender. Major Lewis brings his top horse, Murphy's Bar, for Dora to look after and whilst exercising him she meets Chip, who asks her to ride Copper in the race and not Murphy's Bar.

Steve has noticed that Dora and Chip are becoming good friends and is a little jealous. He does not trust Chip and when Ron 'finds' Murphy's Bar, and brings him home lame, Steve is sure Chip is to blame, only to find out later it was Ron.

Steve and Dora go to Lockwood's Farm and see some ponies being unloaded into a barn. Steve suspects they are New Forest Ponies taken illegally.

On the day of the race Chip tells Dora that if she wins the race, or reports his father about the ponies, Lockwood will starve them.

My Story

Tony Essex called me into his office. He had an idea for a script about people stealing young ponies from the New Forest. Would I go down there and buy some? I asked Andrew Fielder, the famous show jumper, if he would take us but we only had one day to do it in. Andrew was helping us out with transport, horses and training for the jumping scenes at the time.

It was a very early start and we arrived at the sales held on the Beaulieu Road. There is not really much of a car park, and horseboxes and trailers were parked on the grass verges. The grey fencing of the pens looked quite stark, and they were full of ponies of all different sizes and shapes. I asked Andrew to do the bidding, which was held in the bidding ring in the middle. The ring had a very high fence with benches around. I thought some of the ponies looked bewildered and a little lost and I would have liked to bring them all home. We had to go for the smallest, which would give them the appearance of being young – and not spend too much money. We bought the ponies, backed the horsebox up to the special ramp and then loaded them. The box had all the partitions taken out and loads of straw put down. We made sure they had a drink and also got hay as it was about a five-hour journey; we kept stopping to check they were OK. They actually travelled very well considering they had probably never been in a box before.

Gillian Blake (Dora) on Sky and Nigel Crewe (Chip) in a scene from The Challenge

New Forest ponies arriving at Lockwood's

My horse Sky had a bit of a part. She played Murphy's Bar and because Gillian was riding her in wide open spaces, and she had been raced as a two-year old, I put a Pelham on her because she could be hard enough to ride without Gillian having to say lines as well. Gillian did very well and just sat quietly while Sky pranced about.

Dora and Chip prepare for the Challenge

Episode 7: The Letter

Directed by Jack Cardiff

The Story

Dora and Steve are out looking for the New Forest Ponies which Lockwood said he would starve. Mr Plum, the baker, brings his old pony, Georgie, to Follyfoot as he has had to retire because of Pilkington's new modern bakery. Dora has an idea and goes round his old customers and asks them if they would buy Mr Plum's bread, if they deliver it when exercising the horses. Ron calls at the big house which belongs to Mr Pilkington and puts his foot in it as usual. In the meantime, Steve is still looking for the ponies. Ron visits Lockwood's, looks for the ponies and finds them. Chip spots him and gives him a letter for Dora. When Mr Lockwood comes back he catches Ron so he moves the ponies, leaving them in a horsebox on Mr Pilkington's land. Mr Pilkington's daughter, Lisa, falls off her horse as it bolts and comes across the horsebox with the ponies. She tells her dad, who brings them back to Follyfoot Farm.

Mr Pilkington admits his bread is no good and employs Mr Plum to do the baking in a new shop. Steve hands over the letter that Chip wrote, which would give them the evidence to put Lockwood away, but Dora decides she will keep it and only use it against Lockwood if he does it again.

Mr Plum (George Malpas) bringing Georgie to Follyfoot

New Forest ponies arrive at Follyfoot

My Story

When Steve took Georgie to show him Mr Plum's bread round, I was hidden in one of the drives to try to persuade the pony to stop. Once again I got my hand in shot for a split second. I am surprised that Tony Essex did not want my hands chopping off!

Ron did not do much riding in the series so it was decided to let him have Tonto, the black and white horse to ride. Because of Ron's personality he was given a western saddle. We shot quite a lot of film of Ron riding to the different houses asking about Mr Plum's bread. Unfortunately it was all cut out and all you see is Tonto standing behind the Rolls Royce at Mr Pilkington's house.

Tracy, the daughter of Sadie Eddon, did the falling off for Lisa.

Follyfoot Remembered: Tracy Eddon (Stunt Rider)

My parents, Eddie and Sadie, both stunt performers, ran a riding school just outside Windsor in Berkshire. A lot of actors would be sent to our school in order to learn how to ride for a film or television role, so that they would look confident in the saddle for the camera.

My mother had worked on *Follyfoot*, doing stunts that were too dangerous for the cast to undertake. Amongst others, she worked on a *Follyfoot* episode called *Barney*, from the third series, and was dragged around a paddock, at speed, by a wild horse.

When the director wanted a young girl to play the part of Lisa Pilkington in an episode called *The Letter*, my mother suggested me for the role. I was around thirteen at the time, and I travelled up to Yorkshire from London with my parents. I had a couple of scenes to film – one involved trying to control a runaway horse called Sputnik. When filming was completed we all returned to London.

A few weeks later I had a call from the producer to say that they had discovered a fault when the film, including my scenes, had been developed. They wanted me to return to Yorkshire to re-shoot. This time my parents put me on the train in London and I travelled up to Yorkshire alone. I stayed at a bed and breakfast with Arthur English, who looked after me.

I am still a professional stunt woman and continue to work extensively in film and television, from *Star Wars* and *James Bond* to *Midsomer Murders* and *Dr Who*.

Tracy Eddon (far left) filming a scene from The Letter

Episode 8: The Bridge Builder

Directed by David Hemmings

The Story

A gypsy girl called Tina brings her horse, Dado, to Follyfoot Farm because the other four horses are seriously ill. The vet comes, looks at Dado and pronounces him fit. Tina runs off when she sees the headmistress of the local school who has brought some children to be taught riding by Dora. But Dora is worried about the gypsy horses, which are poorly, and she has no idea where they are. Steve has been looking for them but so far no luck. The riding lessons are taking place when suddenly they notice Dado in the lake. When he gets out they follow him to the woods and find Tina, who is eventually persuaded to take them to the Gypsy encampment where the poorly horses are laid down. Steve goes back to Follyfoot for medicines and help. They treat the horses and Dora lends them some of hers, while the sick ones recover at Follyfoot.

Dora sees the headmistress about the gypsy children going to the school and that, even though they are different, they should be treated as well as anybody else at the school. In the meantime, Tina brings the borrowed horses back and says she will help Dora build bridges, by helping teach the children from the school to ride.

The sick horse at the Gypsy camp

My Story

In this episode I was quite horrified that the stunt guys were not only coming to Follyfoot Farm to play the part of the Gypsies, but to train some of our horses to lie down. Only two horses were to be shown on film, so Tonto and Alex got the parts. It was funny really. When Alex was trained he took to it like a duck to water and once down, did not want to get up. When it was tea break, Alex stayed down and allowed you to sit on him and have a cup of tea; he was great. Tonto, whom I thought might be a handful, eventually got used to the idea and lay there as good as gold. The reason we only showed two horses was because the spot where we filmed in the wood, which was by the second little lake at Follyfoot, did not have much room for the caravan, all the cast and of course the crew.

The story of Dado and Hercules. One day we were filming in the yard when suddenly someone shouted, 'horse in the lake'. I thought here goes another joke, then someone said, 'for goodness sake look and see'. Lo and behold, there was Hercules swimming quite happily in

David Hemmings directing

the lake except for one thing – he did not know how or where to get out. I decided to get the old faithful bucket of food and find a place where I thought he would be able to walk out. I found somewhere and called him for all I was worth and, bless him, he came swimming across, got out and ate his food, which he was allowed to have for being such a good boy. We walked up to the stables where he had a good rub down and groom, a nice hot bran mash with treacle to warm him up and a blanket was put on him. I was so thankful that Hercules had not been hurt, and the pike in the lake had not bitten him. I then got a phone call from Tony Essex saying he wanted to put the swimming horse into a script and that we had to teach him to go in the lake on command, and come out at the other side for a feed. I thought, oh dear, why did Hercules have to go in the Lake? We began training the next day. One of the Horse Girls led him in and I went to the other side and called him. He loved it and, if I am honest, he took hardly any training at all. To get the shot a rubber dinghy was used to carry the cameraman and the sound man, and it was pulled across the lake on ropes. We did two takes. On the second take Hercules got his legs tangled in the ropes pulling the dinghy, so it was decided enough was enough. Another story concerns David Hemmings and I. For some reason filming had come to a stand-still and I had a free afternoon. I needed to go to the saddler in Wetherby and David said he would take me because I had never taken a driving test. We were driving along Harewood Avenue when we came across a trailer turned over and a Land Rover at the side of the road. I asked David to stop because I knew who it was and wanted to help if we could. The horses had been taken to some stables down a track and one of them was injured and needed to be stitched. Janet, the owner of the horses, wanted to stay with her horse, and asked us if we could fetch the horsebox as her father was away. I asked David if he could drive a horsebox to which he said 'yes', so off we went. I did not realise that David had done rally driving but we went like the wind to get the box. Janet's mother was waiting for us, gave us the keys and warned us the box had an unusual gear system. David got in the box but, whilst backing out of the garage, hit the guttering and took it off, scratching the box in the process. We then drove to the scene of the accident where the police had now got involved. David said, 'Oh no'. 'What's wrong?' I said, to which he replied, 'I have never driven one of these in my life'. I replied, 'You're a very good actor. Act your way out of this.' But all the police were concerned about was letting us through to get to the horses and get them home so they could receive treatment. To my surprise, the horses went in to the horsebox without a second glance, even after the accident, so we got them home where the vet was waiting. David by this time was beside himself and said he could not watch the horse being stitched and so was taken in the house for a really well deserved drink. I admired David very much for doing what he did. It took courage and it is something I will never forget.

Hercules doubling for Dado

Preparing to film Hercules in the lake

Cameraman filming Hercules in the lake

Follyfoot Remembered: Mervyn Cumming

I was sent out to act as Second Assistant Director on the final series of the show, as a very new Floor Manager. The last series was intended to be a 'run up' for a feature film of Follyfoot, and as such had a film First Assistant, called Ray Frift, and a film production manager, called Ron Liles. I think I was sent out as a peace offering to the A.C.T.T. (Association of Cinematography and Television Technicians) who were very suspicious of the freelance film staff who were being employed. Once the film First and Production Manager accepted that I was there to work, and not just a sop to the union, they were great and I learned a tremendous amount from them, much of which stood me in good stead in subsequent years.

The pressure was enormous, and after a long day of filming we were summoned back to YTV each evening to watch rushes. On several occasions the Producer would keep the Director back after the showing, and the following morning, there would be a new Director on the shoot! 'The Black Taxi' was famous; it used to bring the Producer out to location. We were always warned about its impending arrival by the Production Secretary. Tony Essex was a very strange and obsessive man!

My two most abiding memories both concern the shoots that David Hemmings directed. He had an idea that he wanted to do a tracking shot across the lake as Gillian walked along the bank. Ron Liles and I scoured the area for a pontoon to use as a camera platform, but without success. It was the height of summer and all the marinas that we approached were unable to supply a suitable item.

David was disappointed and, on the Crew Recce before shooting began, bemoaned the fact that he couldn't get the shot he wanted. At this point Roy Buller, one of the Sparks (electricians) said, 'I've got a dinghy in the back of my car'. In great excitement, David then asked to see it and Roy produced this very small child's inflatable dinghy! Ray Frift's eyes went heavenward – this was long before the days of 'Health and Safety', but he could see a disaster waiting to happen.

On the day, the Chippie was sent to cut out a baseboard to insert into the floor of the dinghy, and the process of setting up the shot began. Peter Jackson, not exactly a small

Lynne Frederick (Tina) and Gillian in a scene from The Bridge Builder

Gillian Blake as Dora

person, made larger by his Tensen anorak, and Wellington boots, was inserted into the dinghy with the camera, on its mount, inserted between his knees. The prop boys roped the dinghy stem to stern, and rehearsals began, with them pulling him across the lake, while Gillian did a 'moody' walk along the bank.

Peter complained that he was unable to pan the camera due to the restrictions of space in the dinghy, and so he was brought back to the bank. The ropes were then attached to the sides of the dinghy so that he could face the bank whilst being tracked across the water. Another rehearsal – the dinghy was moving too slowly. At this point, David Hemmings said, 'I'll show you the speed it needs to go!' and went to join the prop boys on the rope pulling the dinghy across the water. The camera was started, the shot marked, and the scene began. David hauled hard on the rope and the side of the dinghy dug into the water. The prop boys on the other rope, seeing this potential disaster, hauled on their rope which was on the other side of the dinghy. The dinghy then flipped over, depositing Peter and the camera into the water. Peter's Tensen became waterlogged, and his Wellingtons filled with water. The Grip, Mel, seeing that his guv'nor was struggling in the water, dived in fully dressed and hauled Peter to the bank – and then went back for the camera!

When he located it, and hauled it up from the bottom of the lake, it was still running! The film magazine was rushed to the laboratories in Leeds because there were other scenes previously shot on the film. When the film was developed, there was no damage at all to it. There was a wonderful shot of the camera descending into the murk, and emerging again – still in perfect focus! But the shot was abandoned, and filmed from the other bank of the lake!

The other tale I recall was one afternoon when we were again shooting by the lake and Gillian was required to walk away from the camera into the sunset.. Finally, the sun was exactly as the Director needed, and the camera turned over. Gillian was cued to walk away from the camera into the sunset. When the Director had the shot he needed, he whispered, 'Cut,' and then, 'That's a tea break.' The crew then silently removed the camera and went in for tea, leaving Gillian still walking into the sunset! When she finally had the nerve to stop and look round, all she saw was an expanse of empty field, with not a soul in sight!

It was a very stressful but hugely enjoyable experience to work on the show. There were, on occasions, huge tensions but also many funny moments. Ask Jane whether she remembers the flatulent horses, who ruined a long tracking shot through the fields. All in all, I learned a tremendous amount on the show; and, as stated before, the lessons which I learned stood me in good stead throughout my career. I also made a considerable amount of money, working huge amounts of overtime!

Episode 9: Uncle Joe

Directed by Peter Hammond

The Story

Two little children, Angela and her brother Jackie, lose their parents in a car accident and Dora, Steve and Ron try to find their only relative, Uncle Joe, who is a very famous show jumper. In the meantime the children are put into an orphanage, from where they run away to Follyfoot Farm to see Champion, their pony. Uncle Joe, thanks to Ron, has been found and is at the Farm and says he will adopt them. Dora finds herself attracted to Joe, which does not please Steve, but Uncle Joe takes Champion and the children home and once again, Dora feels very lonely.

Paul Ambrose (Jackie), Chloe Franks (Angela) and David Hemmings in **Uncle Joe**

My Story

In Slugger's Circus one of the riders is actually Tamara, the daughter of Tony Essex, who found the name Follyfoot and also supported her father in the making of the series.

When filming Slugger's Circus, the ponies attached to the rail pulled the top rail off, as it was quite flimsy, but luckily the Horse Girls were at hand and quickly caught them, so no one was hurt, including the ponies.

The car crash scene was film that was supplied from somewhere else and had been used on quite a few other programmes. In addition, we really did not want to crash a good Jaguar, which would have cost a lot of money plus the price of the stunt.

Gillian was by now doing her own stunts and she did her own jumping. David Hemmings also did his own riding. He must have found it quite difficult because Copper really was too small for him. Copper also, when excited, used to port with his front leg, but Gillian just kept on talking as if nothing was happening. It really must be quite hard to have to act and control a horse that is being a little bit naughty.

Peter Hammond (centre back) directing **Uncle Joe**

Gillian and David between takes

Episode 10: The Helping Hand

Directed by Anthony R Thomas

The Story

Ron is in the barn smoking and sets it on fire, which luckily does not cause too much damage. At the same time Slugger is baking some bread, which also catches fire. The Colonel is away and asks an old friend, Bernard Fox, to keep an eye on Follyfoot Farm. When he goes there to visit he finds lots of faults and says he will send a manager to organise and show them the ropes. Steve and Dora are out riding when they come across a large man with a Shetland pony, called Lollypop. He makes out that he may ride the pony so Dora offers him £25. He also admits to not taking the saddle off for two months.

The manager, Phyllis Wetherby, arrives at Follyfoot Farm to stay but Slugger's food, and a spider in the bath, send her packing to the nearest room in the village. Dora still has to find £25 in order to buy the Shetland, and asks Ron, who says he will think of something.

Phyllis starts work and says that Lancelot, a very old horse, should be put down. She also finds Ron smoking in the barn again and says he must go. Dora asks Steve for help and he tells her she must take control and be Mistress of Follyfoot. Ron gets the money by bringing two horses for schooling, asking for the money in advance, and then goes to get Lollypop. In the meantime Phyllis has arranged for the vet to come and put Lancelot down. Dora says no and tells Phyllis to go and that she is Mistress of Follyfoot. Phyllis then says it was the Colonel's idea, which makes Dora think that he does not trust her.

Ron and Slugger assist the departing Phyllis Wetherby (Aletha Charlton)

My Story

I remember I was horrified when I realised they were really going to set a fire in the barn. We tidied the barn and just put the loose straw in a pile away from anything else, and we had fire-fighting equipment standing by. It actually went well and looked authentic.

Tony Essex wanted Lancelot to really look bad so we got a horse from the knackers yard on loan just for the filming. We all found this quite sad and hoped he enjoyed his remaining days, where we gave him good food and as much love as we had time for.

***Filming* The Helping Hand**

Steve and Dora fighting the fire

Episode 11: Rain on Friday

Directed by Michael Tuchner

The Story

It is raining all day and tempers are running high. Tansy, the pony who had strangles, is not well. Steve is worried that Follyfoot Farm is costing the Colonel too much money and thinks it should be self-sufficient by taking horses in to school. He wants to farm out some of the older horses to make more room. The older horses would go to Mr Chadwick, an ex racehorse-trainer, who is starting up again, and until he gets going is willing to stable some of the Follyfoot horses. Dora has a word with the Colonel about building some more stables and talks to Steve, who is still not happy as he feels he is living on charity. His idea is to send ten ponies to Chadwick's at a cost of £5 each per week and bring to Follyfoot Farm ten ponies for schooling at £10 per week, making a profit of £50.

Steve and Ron end up having a fight in the barn in front of Dora, which the Colonel breaks up. Dora tells the Colonel she has been trying to keep Follyfoot the same as when he ran it. The Colonel then admits to doing exactly what Steve has suggested, and that he started Follyfoot to take the old ponies so his original stables, could become a training yard. Dora decides to let some of the ponies go to Chadwick's.

My Story

Much of this episode was shot indoors and with little horse action, so it was like a holiday for the Horse Girls, well at least from filming and meant we could just enjoy the horses. The rain was faked by the effects team, so we didn't even have to endure bad weather!

It was about this time that we all realised filming and our life at Follyfoot was coming to an end. There were rumours that a feature film might be made, but we were all rather down. I went to drown my sorrows at the Harewood Arms and had to be rescued by Ray Frift (First Assistant to Tony) who gently chided me for walking off set even though there was not much to do.

When I returned with Ray I did not get the expected telling off from Tony. Instead he offered me work on his next project, *Luke's Kingdom*, which was to be filmed in Australia. Tony said that was too far away for me to 'walk out' again! I was tempted, but for personal reasons I did not accept the offer.

Sadly the feature film of *Follyfoot* was never made.

Dora watching the rain

Episode 12: Hazel

Directed by Michael Tuchner

The Story

The Colonel asks Dora round for tea to meet Hazel, who has behaviour problems, and he hopes that Dora will take her on at Follyfoot. Dora thinks she has enough on with Steve without taking Hazel as well. Hazel comes to Follyfoot to have a look round. Dora is upset because Copper has a thorn in his leg and does not want to get involved with Hazel, but Steve, coming from the same sort of background, understands Hazel.

Hazel breaks a picture of Steve's mum and runs away. The police are called and it turns out that as a child, she wanted a pony for her birthday but ended up with a dressing table set. She did everything her foster parents had asked, but the pony never arrived and she was also bullied by other children.

Hazel comes back to Follyfoot Farm to see Steve, in whom she feels she can confide, but then locks Steve in. She gets into Copper's stable with an iron bar but she cannot hurt Copper and sits in the corner, crying. Dora takes pity and realises that Hazel's story is in fact hers and decides that Hazel should take her place at Follyfoot Farm.

Hazel with a Tetley shire horse

Steve looking at the picture of his mother

My Story

The Shire horses came from Tetley's Brewery and the filming of them took place in a field on the Arthington Road, between Harewood and Otley. The Shires were working horses and were still used to pull the brewery drays in Leeds city centre. In fact they were used to deliver beer to my father's former hotel near City Square. They were also a popular draw at local horse shows where they often won prizes. Their Grooms were very proud of their charges and came with the horses, so they were in charge when filming. Sorry to say with the Tetley grooms in charge, there was not much horse action for the girls to get involved in.

I was allowed to take a weekend off and arranged to visit my sister in High Wycombe. One of the crew was also going south and offered to give me a lift.

We were driving on the A1 when we heard a police car siren. I was sitting next to the driver on the bench seat with my arm round his shoulders. He told me to remove my arm as he thought it may be against the law to drive like that. Sure enough the police pulled us in, but to our amazement they knew our names! They said they had received a message that there was an urgent need for us back at YTV, as Tony Essex needed an extra shot for the episode being broadcast that Sunday.

The police escorted us to a phone box so I could phone my sister (who was not pleased by this change of plan), before we turned round and drove back to Leeds.

When we arrived at the YTV studios, the rest of the crew were in the bar oblivious to the reason for our being called back. I ran upstairs to Tony's office to ask what he was playing at. Tony had promised my parents he would look out for me and was angry, because he thought I had gone off for the weekend with the crew member. He had not known I was actually visiting my sister. When she met him some months later she gave him a real telling off!

Veronica Quilligan (Hazel) and Gretchen Franklin (Mrs Porter) in an unused scene from **Hazel**

Episode 13: Walk in the Wood

Directed by David Hemmings

The Story

Clegg's have arrived to build the new stables, and Lancelot is dying. Dora is depressed about the changes taking place at Follyfoot Farm and is still thinking of leaving, but it has to be her decision. Dora is out riding when she sees some young children frightening a pony, goes to stop it and catches one of the little boys. Copper is scared off and runs into the woods. Dora cannot find Copper and rings up the Colonel, who brings some horses to make a search party. Dora has to get back to Follyfoot because Lancelot is dying, but she is too late and Hazel tells her how she had sat with him just as Dora would have done. Copper still cannot be found and the next day Dora and Steve ride out. Steve thinks it's the tinkers and gets the police involved, but the tinkers are not to blame. Steve and Dora have another row and she asks him to leave.

The police bring Copper back to find out that the little boy she captured, had hidden him in a barn and was looking after him until Dora found him. Dora decides to stay and Steve says he needs her more than anyone else in his life. She nods her head to say that he can stay.

My Story

This is the final episode of *Follyfoot* and the story of poor old Lancelot who, when it came to the dying scene, was too big to lie down in the stable and it had to be enlarged to get him and all the crew in. Having done that, there was still not enough room. The stunt man, Tony Smart, had fallen in love with one of the pit ponies, Farmer, who he suggested could double for Lancelot. Farmer played the part of Lancelot so well he did not need a bridle, and we got him to go down with just a head collar and he lay as if he was really dead.

Director David Hemmings wanted to finish the final episode of *Follyfoot* with an aerial shot of the farm taken from a balloon. I remember the weather that last few days was quite poor and that must be why the shot was never made. Such a pity, I would have loved a trip in the hot air balloon!

The three series were now complete. Gillian was already the owner of Copper and I was given a young horse called Tom Jones. Alex went to a riding school and Janet Harrison took several of the horses and one of the new Forest ponies. The remaining horses were bought by a friend of mine who gradually sold them on to suitable homes.

Some years later there was a newspaper article about a horse found swimming in his owner's pool. It was Hercules (Dado) up to his old tricks again!

The terms of filming required that Follyfoot disappear from Hollin Hall completely, and that it was returned to its' original form, though in rather better condition. New owners restored the old farm house, and later still other owners have completely renovated and enlarged the farm.

The final aerial shot of Follyfoot Farm that might have been!

her head, baffled, withdrawing.
Steve starts slowly towards her.

> STEVE: (CHALLENGING, BUT WE KNOW THE ANSWER HE WANTS) Well, what do you want me to do? I need you too, Dora – more than I've ever needed anyone in my life. You're the strong one. You walk in an enchanted wood – and (HE NODS TO THE BOY AND THE WOODMAN) there's your knight in armour, – there's your Gabriel. I was wrong. (PAUSE) You weave miracles, Dora, from the fabric of dreams. I'd give anything to do the same. (PAUSE) Help me.

Dora turns, looks at his earnest anxious face. Slowly she nods. It is an act of sacrifice, for she should do as Ron says, run for her life – but she doesn't. She nods. Steve takes Copper's bridle and leads the horses up the yard. Hazel has been watching, now she comes down and looks at her. Dora sees her, smiles wrily.

> DORA: Don't ever grow up.

She leans tiredly against her tree.

> DORA: I've been for a long walk. (SHE SMILES SADLY) And the Queen was in Australia.

She sighs, puts her head against the tree and feels very, very sorry for herself.

THE END

Actual last page of script, from the final Follyfoot episode – Walk in the Wood

(THIRD SERIES)   FINAL DAY OF SHOOTING — CALL SHEET 67   PROD. NO. 3670- and various others

PRODUCTION: "Follyfoot"
EPISODE: "The Bridge Builder" and pick ups (various Episodes)
DIRECTOR: David Hemmings
DATE: Sunday 3 June 1973
UNIT CALL: 0830
LOCATION: Hollin Hall Farm, Harewood.

ARTISTE	CHARACTER	DRESSING ROOM	MAKEUP/HAIR	SET CALL

1. EPISODE: "Barney" EXT. FIELD/PADDOCK & BARNEY'S SHED Sc. 23Pt(D)

| Gillian Blake | Dora | Follyfoot | 0700 | 0830 |
| Christian Rodska | Stryker | " | 0745 | 0830 |

HORSE:
"Dolly" (doubling for "Barney") via Reg Dent (with Brian Bowes standing by)
PROPS: (via Jane Royston)
Saddle and tack.
WARDROBE NOTE:
Continuity clothes both artistes.

2. EPISODE: "The Long Dark Tunnel" — Riding Sequence EXT. FIELD

| Gillian Blake | Dora | Follyfoot | from above | |
| Michael Greenwood | (riding double for Chip) | " | 0800 | 0830 |

HORSES (via Jane Royston)
"Copper" for Gillian Blake
"Sirocco" for Michael Greenwood } already on site
(doubling horse for original "Brigadier")

WARDROBE NOTE:
Complete continuity.
PROPS:
None required.

3. EPISODE: "The Dream" (Re-take) EXT. FIELD & TRACK (Day for Night)

| Michael Letby | (riding own m/cycle) | | Already on site with the unit | |
| Steve Hodson | Steve (for walking out) | | 0745 | 0830 |

4. EPISODES: Various. Riding and walking shots.

| Gillian Blake | Dora | Follyfoot | from above | |
| Steve Hodson | Steve | " | " | " |

WARDROBE NOTE:
Check for continuity (various shots) with cutting copies on Editing Machine.
HORSES:
As required by Director.

CATERING: (via Kennedys)
Normal breaks all day.
RUSHES:
None today.

Final Follyfoot call sheet, showing re-takes required on the last day of filming

In Conversation with Gillian Blake (Dora)

Where did you audition for the role of Dora?
I auditioned in London for Tony Essex, Peter Jackson and Audley Southcott. Other actresses were also auditioned, including Zoe Wanamaker. When I read for the part, Dora's character of being a sad and lonely girl had already been developed.

Did you film a pilot episode?
Yes, I made a pilot with Robin Stewart playing the part of Paul. The pilot was made to promote the intended series and gauge reaction from the TV networks. When the series was given the go ahead, Robin was replaced by Steve Hodson. Each episode took around ten days to film, and we usually started on

Gillian Blake (Dora)

Gillian with Chloe Franks and David Hemmings, in between scenes from Uncle Joe

Wednesday. If we were filming at Hollin Hall I would usually arrive at 7am, go into costume and makeup and be on set ready to start filming at 8am. We would break for an hours lunch, and then finish around 5pm.

As the series progressed, were you aware how popular the show was becoming?
Yes, we had enormous public reaction, both from the UK and abroad – especially Australia and New Zealand, as well as Germany who co-funded

Gillian behind the camera with lighting cameraman Peter Jackson

the series. I was initially contracted for one series, but when it became evident how successful the series was becoming, and the viewing figures achieved, I was contracted for another series, with an option for a third.

There was a planned *Follyfoot* feature film – do you know what the proposed storyline would have been?
A film script was written by Tony Essex and I have the original which Tony gave to me. I am not sure of the proposed storyline without looking at it again, but it would have continued on from where the final episode – Walk in the Wood – ended. It would have developed the storyline and tied up some of the loose ends, and was going to be made by David Hemmings' production company – Hemdale.

Where did you stay whilst making the series.
I stayed in Yorkshire at the home of Tony Essex and his family, and used to travel home to London on Sunday evening.

Follyfoot won the 1972 Best Children's Drama award from the Society of Film and Television arts. Why do you think the series has become a cult classic?
Follyfoot was non-specific – it had family values, the coveted Sunday teatime slot and horses!

A few years ago there was talk of remaking the series – could it be remade?
Yes it could, but without Tony Essex you wouldn't get the driving force and discipline that he brought to the show. Tony was a workaholic – passionate about the series, and a total perfectionist. As I mentioned, filming for each new episode usually began on a Wednesday and, if after viewing the day's filming, an actor or director didn't come up to the mark they would be dismissed and sent home on the Friday. They became known as the legendary 'Friday night train people!' Tony couldn't drive, so his arrival on set was usually announced by this black taxi cab trundling down the track to the farm, usually followed by a swirling dust storm!

Did you manage to see any of the series when it was shown?
Yes, as well as watching the daily rushes back at the Yorkshire Television studios, I used to watch the episodes on Sunday afternoon before leaving Yorkshire to go home to London. I have recently bought the series on DVD, but have not got around to watching it yet!

Does any particular episode or scene stay in your memory?
I remember Out of the Blue Horse from the second series, which was directed by Peter Hammond. Peter himself was once an actor, and he also directed me in two other dramas

that I did after Follyfoot – *Hallelujah, Mary Plumb* and *The Happy Autumn Fields. Out of the Blue Horse* was a really difficult and demanding episode to film. It was a heartbreaking story written by Tony Essex and by the end I was totally exhausted, but I enjoyed every single minute of it. I remember another episode also from series two called

Robin Stewart and Gillian in an early publicity photograph

The Innocents. *The story was set around a miner's strike, and Dora thought that pit ponies had been abandoned down the mine. The episode was directed by Desmond Davis who wanted to film inside the actual mine, but this proved too dangerous. Instead a set was built of the inside of the mine, and most of the filming at the top of the mine was done late at night, to keep the atmosphere as realistic as possible.*

Did you ever revisit the farm after the series ended?
I did go back a few years later when I was in Yorkshire with my husband Peter. That was the only time, although I have seen some recent pictures of how the farm and stables look today.

What happened to *Copper*?
I was given Copper *whilst making the series, and when it ended took him home with me. He was stabled in the garden and I rented a field just down the road. He lived until he was*

Gillian riding Copper Prince

twenty-five, when his back legs started to give problems, which is a very good age for a part Arab. He also appeared with me in a one-off TV drama called Can You Keep a Secret? that was made in 1976 by Anglia, and shown on the ITV network.

You shared a lot of very dramatic scenes with Steve Hodson – how did you get along with him?

We got along just great, and in fact appeared on stage together in some plays after the series ended.

You've appeared in Film, TV and on stage – do you have a preferred medium?

I prefer TV. With film you do the job and then move on. With a stage run it's a lot of repetition doing the same play night after night. On Follyfoot I was interested and fascinated by the technical aspects, and was always asking Peter Jackson (Lighting Cameraman) why he was shooting a scene from that angle, or why was he lighting the scene this way or that way.

Gillian Blake on 'Ron's motorbike'

37 Years Later

One night in August 2007, I received a phone call asking me if I was the Jane who had worked at Yorkshire Television on the *Follyfoot* series. I said yes, but it was many years ago. The caller introduced himself as Ray Knight from Bournemouth.

Ray told me that *Follyfoot* was very big on the Internet and also a DVD had come out of the first series, and that the second series would be coming out the following year.

Ray told me he had arranged to visit Yorkshire to meet Peter Jackson, the Cameraman on *Follyfoot,* but sadly Peter had died. I asked Ray to come anyway and I could show him some of the locations. I found Ray was really nice to talk to, especially about *Follyfoot*. He seemed to love the programme very much and had a great knowledge, more than I did.

I discussed with Ray that I had been thinking about writing a book, which would explain the way the programme came about and tell the behind-the-scenes stories that happened while making the programme. In addition, there were a lot of private photographs which had never been seen before. Ray seemed very excited about the prospect.

Ray came up in September and we went to Follyfoot Farm, to look at the old stable buildings. I found it quite sad. We then went to Ilkley where we did some filming for the *Steve* episode, then to Eagle Hall at Pately Bridge which was used in a couple of episodes. The next day Ray wanted to find the Lock Keeper's Cottage and where we did the scenes by the canal. Sadly, I failed miserably on this – we did not even get down to the canal. However, we did find some of the other locations in Wetherby, Thorner, Sicklinghall and Little Ribston. It really was a good fun weekend.

Ray and I kept in touch putting the book together, and we contacted the stars and people who worked on the series, to contribute to the book. Ray rang me one evening to say he had been looking on the Internet and had seen a request by a Television Producer, Dee Marshall. She wanted to talk to anyone who had worked on *Follyfoot* or was a keen fan to contact her, as she was making a documentary on locations in Yorkshire used in films and television. Ray and I discussed it and decided it might be a good idea, to get involved. I contacted Dee and arranged a meeting.

Dee came to see me and seemed pleased that she had found me, as I was the one who had found the *Follyfoot* location and had a story to tell about it. It was arranged that I would take part in the film and also to ask Ray if he would take part, which I knew he would love to do. We were told that the person who would interview us would be John Middleton – Ashley, the vicar in *Emmerdale* – and that he was very nice and easy to get on with.

The day of filming arrived. Both Ray and my sister, Ann, had come to stay. Dee had managed to contact a cameraman, Charlie Flynn, a sound guy, Ron Atkinson, and the continuity

Filming 'Lights, Camera, Location' at Follyfoot Farm

lady, Anne Ayoub, to be interviewed as well as Ray and myself. At lunchtime we went to the Harewood Arms, where Ann Ayoub joined us. It really did seem funny seeing her again and I thought she had not altered much at all.

We got to Follyfoot Farm for 1pm and met the camera crew and John Middleton. It was funny because I felt I already knew him. I was to be filmed first in the yard, which sadly had changed and did not resemble Follyfoot Farm as I remembered it. I was given a sock as my marker to stand on and I tried to forget the camera was there and that I was just having a conversation with a friend, who wanted to know about *Follyfoot*. I nearly got the giggles at one time when the producer wanted close up shots of John asking the questions. I had to stand in the same position as the original take, but not answer. He asked the questions and nodded his head as if I were answering – I had to look down otherwise I would have giggled.

Ray Knight

John Middleton and Jane at Hollin Hall, filming **Lights, Camera, Location**

Radio Leeds

The Graham Liver Show, 10.45am, Friday 15 August

The Story of How This Came About

My friend Lucille was listening to Radio Leeds – the Graham Liver Show, when she heard the word *Follyfoot*. Graham was asking what special animal that had appeared on the television or radio did they like. The phone rang and a guy call Don came on air, saying he used to drive the coach for the cast on *Follyfoot* and his favourite horse was Black Beauty.

Lucille my friend rang me and asked me about it. I replied there was a pony called Black Beauty, which was his real name, and he played the part of Domino in the *Four Legged Hat* episode. I could not get through to Radio Leeds, so I rang Lucille who did it for me and explained the above to them and also that I was writing a book. Radio Leeds rang her back and asked if she thought I would be interested in coming on the show. She told them I would, and they would ring Don, so he could talk to me.

Radio Leeds contacted me and asked me to be on the show Friday 15th August, and I agreed. I must admit I felt very nervous and a little sick as this was going to be live, but I just had to get on with it. Friday arrived and Lucille kept ringing me in the morning, really excited about the response Graham seemed to be getting, as he kept advertising the fact I was coming on and asking for anyone to contact him with any questions or information.

The taxi had arrived to pick me up and I felt sick again with nerves and also I got a frog in my throat. This was a good start! I arrived at the studios, went into reception and immediately asked for a glass of water. Jonathan, the producer, came down to meet me and take me to the production office next to the studio where Graham Liver was broadcasting. I had another drink of water and hoped everything would be OK. Jonathan took me to where Graham was and introduced me and then, hey presto, the theme tune *The Lightning Tree* came on. His first question was, 'You will know all the words to this', to which my answer was 'No!' I felt the interview went quite well and thank heavens my frog had disappeared!

Arthur English Remembered

Arthur was born in Aldershot, Hampshire, and played the loveable, 'Slugger' Jones in *Follyfoot*.

His stage career began in 1949 when he passed an audition at London's Windmill Theatre, and became their resident comedian. Arthur was probably best known for his comical 'spiv' character in the early 1950s, with his big jacket and his flashy long tie, but in *Follyfoot*, he realised his first ambition – acting in straight drama.

Arthur also became a very talented artist, starting with portraits, and then moving on to landscapes.

In 1978 Arthur was the subject of the television programme *This Is Your Life*, with guest appearances from both Gillian Blake and Steve Hodson. In 1986 his autobiography, *Through The Mill and Beyond*, was published.

Arthur never auditioned for the role as Slugger in *Follyfoot*. Tony Essex and his team were watching an episode of a comedy called *Bless This House*, primarily to look for a candidate for the role of Steve. In this particular episode, Arthur had a small role as a traffic warden and when Tony and his team saw him they all agreed – that is Slugger!

In *Follyfoot*, Slugger, who was the Colonel's ex-batman and a former boxer, was also known for his notorious lack of cooking skills – bacon and eggs or stew! Slugger provided the comic relief during the series, which nicely balanced the more intense relationship between Dora (Gillian Blake) and Steve (Steve Hodson).

Arthur's comedy timing was very much in evidence in his scenes with Christian Rodska (Ron Stryker). Although his father was a professional jockey, Arthur was not a horseman. He was quite happy tending to the two resident Follyfoot donkeys – Bubble and Squeak – but not so keen on being too close to horses.

In one of his very first scenes, directed by Frederic Goode, Arthur had to wait by the Follyfoot gate for Desmond Llewelyn to come riding up on his horse. Arthur had to hold the horse, wait for Desmond to dismount and then lead it into the stable yard. Seeing this massive horse up close, nerves got the better of Arthur, and he turned round and fled. The scene had to be re-shot, and from that moment on his character, Slugger, was allowed to refer to his four legged friends as 'orrible great brutes!'

Arthur English – a talented artist

Desmond Llewelyn Remembered

Desmond Llewelyn played Colonel Geoffrey Maddocks in *Follyfoot*, the uncle of Dora, whom she goes to stay with whilst her parents are abroad. As well as his large country estate, the Colonel also owns Follyfoot Farm – a home of rest for tired, unwanted and neglected horses.

Desmond had a long and distinguished career, in stage, television and film, but is perhaps best known as 'Q' in the *James Bond* films. His agent put his name forward for the part of the Colonel in *Follyfoot*. He went for a screen test – and got the part.

He loved every moment of being on the show, and worked with Bond actor Bernard Lee in the final *Follyfoot* episode – *Walk in the Wood*. He also worked with director Michael Apted on a couple of episodes – *Moonstone* and *Poor Bald Head*. Years later he would work with him again whilst making the Bond film - *The World Is Not Enough*.

Whilst filming *Follyfoot*, Desmond and his wife rented a small cottage in Sicklinghall, not far from the farm location. When he had any free time he and his wife enjoyed exploring the Yorkshire countryside.

By prior arrangement he was written out of *Follyfoot* during filming of the third series for three episodes, to work on the Bond film *Live and Let Die*. However, Desmond was annoyed by this because in the end they decided not to use him.

Desmond inherited his love of horses from his mother, who insisted that he had a pony, and learned to ride at an early age; this proved useful when he auditioned for the role of the Colonel.

In 1995, Desmond was featured on *This Is Your Life*, which included a guest appearance from Gillian Blake and Christian Rodska. In 1999 Desmond's book *Q, The Biography of Desmond Llewelyn* was published.

The iconic white entrance gates as they are today at Stockeld Park

PHOTOGRAPH CREDITS

All photographs are copyright ©Yorkshire Television with the following exceptions:

The Very Beginning	Jane with Sky © IPC Media
My Follyfoot Journey	Horse Girls Painting © Christine Saul
My Journey with Hollin Hall	Hollin Hall as Follyfoot © Stephanie Kleinman
My Dream becomes a Reality	Me moving in © Christine Saul
	Flash with Susan © Christine Saul
	Christine on Dart Removal. © Christine Saul

SERIES ONE

Episode 1	Stockeld Park © Ray Knight
	Dora's first view of Follyfoot Farm © Stephanie Kleinman
	Remaining photographs © Private Collection
Episode 4	Billy Bland arriving at Follyfoot © Christine Saul
Episode 12	Gillian on Copper © Christine Saul
Christian Rodska Interview	Jack Cardiff and Arthur English © Steve Hodson

SERIES TWO

Episode 1	The same location 40 years later © Ray Knight
Episode 3	Me after telephoning Harvey Smith © Steve Hodson
Episode 12	Attaching my Moustache © Anthony Andrews
	Me as Lord Beck © Anthony Andrews

SERIES THREE

Episode 3	Stunt rider with Barney © Christine Saul
Episode 8	Hercules as Dado © Christine Saul
	Preparing to film Hercules © Christine Saul
	Cameraman filming Hercules © Christine Saul
37 Years Later	Ray Knight © Jane Royston
	Filming Lights, Camera Location © Ray Knight
Desmond Llewelyn	Stockeld Park Gates © Ray Knight

AFTERWORD

I really hope you enjoyed reading all about my memories of *Follyfoot* and how it holds a special place in my heart. If you want to learn more and join a very friendly fans forum, please log on to:

www.follyfoot.co.uk

Thank you.
Jane Royston